MAKING THE MOVE

MAKING THE MOVE

A Practical Guide to
Senior Residential Communities

LETTICE STUART

AVON BOOKS ◆ NEW YORK

MAKING THE MOVE is an original publication of Avon Books. This work has never before appeared in book form.

AVON BOOKS
A division of
The Hearst Corporation
1350 Avenue of the Americas
New York, New York 10019

Copyright © 1997 by Lettice Stuart
Interior design by Kellan Peck
Cover art by Linda Gist
Published by arrangement with the author
Visit our website at http://www.AvonBooks.com
ISBN: 0-380-78981-7

Library of Congress Cataloging in Publication Data:

Stuart, Lettice.
  Making the move : a practical guide to senior residential communities / Lettice Stuart.
    p. cm.
  Includes index.
  1. Life care communities—United States. 2. Congregate housing—United States. 3. Old age homes—United States. 4. Aged—Services for—United States. 5. Moving, Household—United States. I. Title.
HV1454.2.U6S78   1997   96-47039
362.6'1—dc21   CIP

First Avon Books Trade Printing: April 1997

AVON TRADEMARK REG. U.S. PAT. OFF. AND IN OTHER COUNTRIES, MARCA REGISTRADA, HECHO EN U.S.A.

Printed in the U.S.A.

OPM   10 9 8 7 6 5 4 3 2

Dedicated to Mom and Dad
Grace and Perseverance

Acknowledgments

This book could not have been written without the help of many people. First and foremost, I want to thank my husband Walter, my daughter Courtney, and my son Burke for their generous love and support. Walter's enthusiasm about the book from the beginning, his constant encouragement, his analytical mind, and his willingness to read and reread each word helped me through many rough spots. Courtney was my cheerleader and research assistant. Her belief in me has often been stronger than my belief in myself. There are many things in my life that I wouldn't have done without Courtney prodding me on. I thank Burke for his silent suffering through my moods during his last year in high school and for teaching me by example about courage and determination.

Special thanks to my sister, Marjorie Roniger, for her social work expertise; my brothers, Dr. Clem Binnings, for his medical expertise, and Tom Binnings, for his financial and business expertise. They each read the manuscript and offered advice. Thanks also to my Aunt Polly Burke, who at age eighty-nine inspired me with her energy, wisdom, and perspective on life.

I owe a special debt of thanks to my dear friends Anne and Barry Munitz. Without their help, advice, and encouragement this book wouldn't have gotten past the idea stage.

I also want to thank my friends Kippy Comfort, Sheila Gaissett, Tim Smith, Lois Ann Peckham, Cindy

Shealor, Claudia Bryan, Molly Malone, Marshall Ashmore, Liz Spradling, and Laura Bacon for their advice and recommendations. I thank my friend and computer adviser Bob Shealor for pulling me out of computer hell by retrieving chapter six after I killed it.

Thanks also to the many people who shared their knowledge with me: Mary Ann Lang, Ted Hodges, Mark Spradling, Andy Billip, Mary Vineyard, Susan Talley, Campbell Palfrey, Kate Salmen, Nancy Kelly, Joe Helms, Harvey Michaels, Jean Copeland, J. B. Gouger, Mel Gamzon, Kirk Gulledge, and Richard Campbell.

And, of course, I thank my agent, Judith Riven, for her enthusiastic support and help.

Contents

Introduction:
What This Book Is About

The idea for this book began with a single question: "When the time comes for you or your aging parent to move from home to some type of senior residential facility, where will you turn for information?"

The question was simple enough, but the answer was not. In recent years a number of books that deal with retirement and other senior-related topics have been published. Many spend a chapter or two discussing residential facilities or communities, but none deals exclusively with the subject. A variety of organizations and associations publish pamphlets and booklets on different types of residential facilities available today, but how does the average consumer know where to write or call for this information? And *what* is a senior residential facility, anyway?

Senior residential facility is really just a catch-all phrase for a new breed of retirement community that provides housing, services, amenities, and health care in a variety of combinations. Not long ago choices for seniors were limited to the two ends of what is now a spectrum of choices—they either stayed at home or moved in with a family member or moved into a nursing home. Fortunately, that's no longer true. Seniors now have a wide range of housing options, but sorting them out can be difficult.

What do the terms "assisted living," "independent

living," "skilled nursing," and "life care" mean? Should you choose a rental or condominium facility, or one that charges an entrance fee? How does an entrance fee work? What should you look for and what questions should you ask when you visit a facility? What are the emotional, psychological, financial, and legal factors to consider? And where will you find answers to these questions?

That's the problem faced by millions of Americans each year as our population ages in record numbers. Thanks to advanced medical technology and the aging of the baby boom generation, our senior population is increasing dramatically. From 1900 until today the number of Americans age sixty-five years or older has grown from 3 to 32 million. By the year 2030, there will be an estimated 66 million senior citizens making up nearly one-quarter of the nation's population!

It's no wonder that senior housing has emerged as one of this country's major concerns. Traditionally, adult children have cared for aging parents, but that's less likely today. With higher divorce rates, more women joining the work force, and adult children moving more frequently in search of job opportunities and advancement, elderly parents are having to seek other alternatives.

In the last decade, the senior housing industry has refocused its efforts to address these concerns. The result is an ever-increasing number and variety of senior residential facilities.

That's the good news. The bad news is twofold. There is very little consumer information on the topic, and what information can be found is confusing because of the industry's failure to develop a consistent terminology. An entrance fee may be called a *founder's fee* or an *endowment fee*. Assisted living is also called *personal care, catered living,* and nearly a dozen other names.

The purpose of this book, therefore, is to solve the problem of where to turn for information when the time comes for you or a family member to move from home to a senior residential facility. Not only does this book explain the concept and define the terms, but it also includes resources, helpful checklists, things to look for, and questions to ask. It is written for both seniors and their adult children, who often find themselves, willingly or unwillingly, cast in the decision-making role when the time comes for a move.

This is not a book about nursing homes, though nursing care as a component of a residential facility is included. Nor is the topic of low-income housing addressed here. Instead, this book focuses on a specific segment of the senior population for whom private-pay senior residential facilities are an option. Various legal and financial issues are raised, but readers are advised to seek professional advice on those matters.

Making the Move is laid out as a step-by-step guide through the moving process. You've already taken the first important step of gathering information. The rest of the process will unfold in the following chapters. Remember that moving will take time and effort, but most seniors and their adult children find the rewards at the end of the journey well worthwhile. Good luck!

MAKING THE MOVE

CHAPTER ONE

Making the Decision

In an ideal world couples would begin thinking about moving to some type of senior residential facility while they are still healthy and vigorous, maybe in their late sixties or early seventies. After spending time researching options, visiting facilities, and talking to people, they would choose the place best suited to meet their present and future housing and health-care needs. Knowing they are sparing themselves and their children considerable stress and anxiety in later years, they would make the move now while they still have their health and each other. Together they would have time to make new friends, develop new interests, and adapt to a new lifestyle before having to cope with illness or the death of a spouse.

This is not an ideal world, however, and most seniors either delay the decision as long as possible or avoid a decision altogether until it is forced on them by a crisis or a family member. Unfortunately, the results are usually less than satisfying. Consider the following situations:

THE DELAYED DECISION

Mom and Dad have been talking for several years about moving into a nearby residential facility where a number of their friends live. Mom really wants to move. She likes the place and thinks it would be fun to live with their friends. Dad, however, is not ready to give up the house and keeps putting off making a decision. Then Dad has a stroke and is left partially paralyzed and confined to a wheelchair. Mom can't care for him alone, but now they can't move to the residential facility where their friends are. That facility restricts entrance to residents who can walk and live independently. The facility has both assisted living and nursing care for residents already living there, but it doesn't admit residents directly to either of those levels.

If only they had moved before Dad's stroke, they could go into the facility's assisted-living section where Mom could get help caring for Dad while still being able to socialize with and receive support from her friends. Now their choices are limited, and Mom is fearful about the future. She is also angry at Dad for not moving sooner and harbors guilt about those feelings.

THE CRISIS DECISION

After falling and breaking her hip, Mom realizes she can't take care of herself without assistance. Around-the-clock care at home is too costly, but Mom knows she can't live with her daughter, a single mother working full time, and she doesn't want to move in with her son 1,000 miles away. What will happen when she's discharged from the hospital next week?

Mom is anxious and depressed about her condition and feels guilty that her daughter will have to shoulder the burden of finding a place for her to live. Her daughter feels guilty that she can't take Mom in, but she's also resentful toward both her brother and Mom that she is the one bearing all of the responsibility. And now she finds out that the facility where she thinks Mom will be the happiest and the best cared for has a waiting period of up to a year because the demand for space there is so high.

THE FORCED DECISION

Dad's vision is failing and his forgetfulness increasing. He's fallen several times and nearly set the house on fire recently when he left a pot on the stove. After trying a variety of different caretaking arrangements, his children intervene and tell Dad that he simply must move into a residential facility where assistance and supervision are provided. Dad is angry at his children and feels he has lost control over his life. The children feel guilty about their decision and guilty that none of them is able or willing to have Dad come live with them. They fight with each other, and they are angry at Dad for putting them in this position.

Whether or not a move to a residential facility is successful depends in large part on who makes the decision, when and under what circumstances the decision is made. Not surprisingly, those who make the decision for themselves and take the time to plan and prepare for the move are the happiest residents. Those who are pushed into a decision by others have the most difficulty adjusting.

Those who wait until a crisis forces them to make the decision often find their options limited. If you wait until you need a walker to get around, you eliminate many facilities that require that residents be ambulatory upon entrance. If you wait until you're lying in a hospital bed with an illness or injury and need to find a place to move to when discharged, you eliminate places that have waiting lists and may be forced into a hasty decision that you have little or no control over.

But why is this such a difficult decision? Why do the vast majority of seniors prefer to stay in their homes despite fear of crime, health worries, feelings of isolation, and the physical and financial strain of maintaining a home?

The reasons are many, but chief among them are

- Denial
- Fear
- Depression and/or grief
- Resistance to change
- Emotional attachment to home
- Lack of knowledge about options

Understanding why the decision is difficult will not make the decision any easier, but it may be a first step in helping both seniors and their adult children communicate with each other about this difficult task.

Denial

Denial or the refusal to accept reality is a common response to painful or highly stressful situations. What could be more stressful than thinking about the possibility of becoming ill and frail and needing care? What could be more painful than the notion of our own mortality or that of a loved one? The elderly, as well as their adult children, often find it easier to deny reality than to think about and plan for the future.

Fear

While many elderly people admit to being afraid in their own homes (afraid of crime and afraid of becoming ill or injured and unable to get help), the thought of moving may be even more threatening. Fears about a residential facility include the fear of the unknown, the fear of being abandoned, the fear of being isolated from family and friends, and the fear of the loss of independence and loss of control over one's own life.

Mom may be afraid to go out after dark, afraid to open her door, and afraid she'll fall in the tub and not be found for days, but at least home is familiar and comfortable. Familiarity is its own security. Perhaps she's shy and afraid to make new friends, or perhaps she's afraid of losing her privacy in a community of so many people.

Depression and/or Grief

Both depression and grief are physically and emotionally depleting and can leave people incapable of making decisions. Whatever the cause of depression— a chemical or hormonal imbalance, prescription drugs, alcohol, grief, illness, or some other stressful situation— it is often immobilizing. Even a mildly depressed person may lack the physical and mental energy necessary to plan a move, much less carry it out.

Remember that grief need not be the result of a specific loss or event such as the death of a spouse or friend. People also grieve over the more gradual or less obvious losses in their lives such as the loss of youthfulness, the loss of their health, and the loss of hopes and dreams for the future. There is also anticipatory grief that occurs ahead of time. Just thinking about moving may cause Dad to begin grieving about his own mortality. Even though he knows a move is the best thing, he may be too incapacitated by grief to make a decision.

Resistance to Change

Elderly people who have experienced many changes in their lives, changes over which they have no control, tend to resist those changes that they can control.

Mom can't keep her hair from graying, her vision from failing, her bones from weakening. She couldn't keep Dad from dying and leaving her alone, but now she can control where she's going to live. Her children think she should move, but that's one change she's not going to make!

Besides, change is stressful and the new is unfamiliar. Mom fears that her slower mental and physical reflexes and her vision loss will make it even more difficult for her to adapt to a new environment, make new friends, and cope with new situations.

Emotional Attachment to Home

Whether you own or rent your home, it is *your* space, your haven from the world. Your home establishes your personal boundaries within which you have a sense of autonomy, control, security, familiarity, and privacy.

Your home is filled with your things and your memories. As you age and watch the future dwindle and the past expand, you strengthen your grip on those memories. It is through your memories that you relive your life. It's hard to let go!

Mom and Dad know that they can't keep up the house and yard the way they used to and that they can't afford to pay someone to do it for them. They know they are spending too much on utilities and property taxes, but how can they leave the house where they raised their four beautiful children and shared such a wonderful life together? The kids have moved away and have their own lives now, but each day this house evokes memories of their times together as a family.

Lack of Knowledge About Options

The greatest misconception about senior residential facilities is that they are cold, sterile, institutional places filled with old people passing time while waiting to die. Many seniors have such little knowledge about senior residential facilities that they equate them with institutional nursing homes—places where people are put rather than places they choose to live. They imagine dreary, confining places where residents are cut off from family and friends and have little if any control over their own lives.

There are ways, however, to help family members through this difficult decision-making process and to help break down their resistance to the idea of moving. The first and most important step is open and honest communication. Discuss your fears and feelings about the situation with your family members and ask them about theirs. It may take some prodding. You might have to ask Mom over and over, "What are you afraid of?" She might tell you ten times that she's not afraid of anything, that she just doesn't want to move. She'll probably get angry. But the eleventh time you ask, she might surprise even herself by saying, "I'm afraid no one will ever come visit me." At least once you've identified her fears, whether they are rational or irrational, you can begin to address the issue and give her the reassurance she needs. In doing so, it is important to acknowledge and respect her feelings.

"Mom, I know you are worried. I know Aunt Jane has said so many times that no one ever came to see her once she moved, but that doesn't mean your children and friends will treat you the same way. Think about it, Aunt Jane was an old biddy and she really didn't have any friends *before* she moved. So many people love you, I assure you that that won't change just because you move to a new home."

For many seniors financial worries are a major cause of fear and anxiety. Again, communication is essential, even though money is a difficult subject for some people. Sit down with your spouse or parent and list all income and expenses. Mom may think there's no way she can afford to live in a residential facility, but when she sees on paper what it costs to maintain the place she lives now, she may discover it would be cheaper to move. Remember that what may seem like a high monthly cost at most residential facilities usually includes all utilities (except telephone), meals, housekeeping, and a variety of services, including transportation. It's possible that Mom doesn't really like to drive but has been keeping her car so she won't feel trapped alone at home. She might choose to get rid of her car and save the high cost of insurance if she's living in a place that provides transportation and includes many conveniences such as a pharmacy, bank, and dry cleaners on-site.

If you're trying to help a reluctant spouse or parent make the decision to move, it is important to express your own fears. The motivating factor for a man who refuses to consider his own physical and emotional well-being may be his wife's fear of being alone one day or his son's anxiety about his father's safety.

Even when dealing with a reluctant spouse or parent, it's important to include the person making the move in the decision-making process as early on as possible. However, an initial meeting with other family members involved may be advisable in an effort to present a united front. You don't want the parent or spouse to feel that the whole family is conspiring behind his or her back, any more than you want one child siding with a parent against the rest of the family. That can be quite destructive.

Soliciting the help of trusted friends or professionals outside of the family circle is often helpful. Ask Mom's clergyman or long-time family doctor to talk to her about making a move. If Mom has a friend who is happy in a residential facility or if you have a friend whose parent has made a successful move, ask their advice and encourage Mom to talk to and even visit them in their homes.

Depression is a common problem among the elderly. A depressed person has difficulty making small decisions, much less such momentous ones such as moving to a residential facility. If your parent or spouse is depressed, try to determine the cause of the depression and seek professional help. Don't assume that Dad's grief over Mom's death is the sole cause of his depression. Explore other possible sources for his mood.

Remember, too, that prescription and other drugs, including alcohol, taken alone or in combination can cause depression. Gather all of his current medications and take them to your pharmacist or doctor to discuss possible side effects. Ask specifically about depression. It's best to take the actual prescription bottles, rather than making a list, so that the doctor or pharmacist can readily determine the precise formulas and dosages. If the doctor isn't helpful, find another one, preferably a geriatric specialist.

Encourage Dad to join a support group to help him deal with his grief. If the depression continues or becomes incapacitating or life threatening, seek professional counseling.

Whether you are considering a move yourself or helping a family member, you need to have a clear understanding of what options are available. Visiting different facilities is the only way to do this, but plan these visits carefully. If your spouse or parent is resistant to the idea of moving, scout out a few places first. Suppose you finally convince your husband to at least *look* at a place you've heard about, and the place turns out to be a disaster. Starting off on the wrong foot may close the subject for good. Cancel the visit if he's not feeling well that day or if the weather is rainy and depressing. Weather is an important factor many people overlook. Naturally, springtime visits are optimal, but at least be sure you visit on a day when the sunshine will brighten the interior and residents will be outside enjoying the outdoor amenities as well.

Schedule the visit for the time of day that your husband's energy level is at its peak. Also consider peak activity hours at the place you'll be visiting. Why visit right after lunch when residents are either out, napping, or sitting around sluggishly? Wouldn't it be better to arrive in the morning when everyone is engaged in some activity or during the late afternoon social hour? Even if you or your husband don't like this particular place, your first impression of life at a residential facility is critical.

Forewarn the person with whom you schedule your visit that your husband will be a reluctant visitor and don't hesitate to offer a few tips on the best way to approach him. After all, who knows his personality quirks better than you?

Another mistake to avoid is taking a reluctant visitor to a facility under construction. Not many people can visualize concrete block walls and cement floors as their home.

If you're taking Mom to visit a place in a neighborhood unfamiliar to her, show her how close it is to your house or some other landmark that she can relate to. During the visit, point out homey, familiar features such as the same rose color of her dining room and the perfect spot at the window for her desk. Let her know that you'll be there to help her move and get settled.

And finally, the most important tool you need to help you through this decision-making process is knowledge. Read on!

CHAPTER TWO

Understanding the Options

Chapter One dealt with the emotional aspects of making the decision to move yourself or a family member to a senior residential facility. This chapter will deal with another integral part of the decision-making process—understanding the options.

How can you decide to move without first understanding what kinds of places you might move to? Few people understand the different choices available today. For most people, the mere mention of a residential facility automatically brings to mind an image of the dreaded institutional nursing home filled with incapacitated old people near the end of their lives. Fortunately, that concept is as outdated as the notion that life ends after retirement.

Because people are living longer, healthier, and more active lives, a huge industry has evolved around the business of providing seniors with places to live. This new breed of retirement facility offers a wide variety of services, housing, and health-care options, all aimed at enhancing the quality of seniors' lives.

Trying to understand the choices, however, can be mind-boggling. Just as most businesses have their own lingo, so does the senior housing industry. The industry's failure to develop a consistent lexicon has resulted in confusion for the consumer. What is called *assisted living* by some is called *personal care* or *catered living* by others. An *entrance fee* is sometimes referred to as an *endowment fee* or *founder's fee*. And to further complicate the situation, a single facility may combine and overlap different levels of care, services, and fee structures.

But take heart. It's not really that complex once you understand several basic terms and concepts. This chapter will define the terms, explain the concepts, and give examples.

The Building Block Model

The biggest obstacle to understanding senior residential facilities is that they cannot be divided into neat categories. Certainly no two places look alike, and neither do they act alike. So rather than try to categorize the whole, we'll categorize the pieces or the similar elements that define these communities.

Imagine a child's set of interlocking building blocks with which you're going to build a residential facility. The blocks are divided into two piles. One pile contains levels of care and the blocks are marked: *Independent Living, Assisted Living,* and *Nursing Care.*

The blocks in the other pile are marked: *Rental, Purchase,* and *Entrance Fee.* They represent methods of payment. You can combine the blocks in any way; your imagination is the only limitation!

You might build a single high-rise building—all assisted living and all rental. You might build a high-rise with some floors for independent living, some assisted living, and some nursing care and charge an entrance fee. Maybe instead, you choose to spread your community out on a campus setting around a lake with trees and walking paths. Along the lake shore you have some independent living cottages that residents purchase as condominiums. Nestled back in the trees you build a high-rise building of rental apartments for assisted living. Between the two you build a one-story nursing facility.

You get the idea! Every residential community has its own identity, but if you understand the different components—the building blocks—you understand the concept. So now let's look at the two sets of blocks: levels of care and methods of payment.

The First Set of Blocks: Levels of Care

The following terms are essential to an understanding of senior residential facilities.

- Independent living
- Assisted living
- Nursing care

Although these terms are applied to the physical units in a community (cottages, town houses, apartments, rooms), they actually refer to the level of care provided to the residents of those units.

INDEPENDENT LIVING

Independent living is the easiest concept to understand. It refers to the ability of active and healthy seniors to live without assistance. Some independent-living communities provide only minimal services such as building and grounds maintenance; others provide an array of services. The residential units may be rented on a monthly basis or owned as condominiums or cooperatives. (Condominiums and cooperatives are explained on pages 20–21.)

Everyone has heard of, if not seen, a retirement community of detached homes, town houses, and apartments built around a golf course or a lake. That's the most obvious example of independent living. The community provides security, grounds maintenance, and possibly a few other services. Basically, it is no different from other residential enclaves, except that all the people who live there are age sixty or older.

That same concept can be applied to a condominium or rental apartment building in an urban area. Here the amenities might include a health club, swimming pool, and concierge. The apartments may be designed with seniors in mind with such features as tub grab bars and emergency call systems, but the distinguishing feature of the community is really the age of its residents.

Independent living is not a new concept. Though retirement communities have been around for years, their construction increased dramatically in the 1970s and early 1980s as developers began to focus on the growing number of senior citizens in this country. Many of those projects failed, however, because developers did not understand two important facts about seniors.

First, most seniors move only when forced to by a crisis such as an illness or the death of a spouse. It was more difficult than developers realized to attract residents because most seniors prefer the emotional security of the home they've lived in for many years.

Second, the turnover rate was high because even most healthy, active seniors eventually need some health-care and support services. The decline of physical abilities is inherent in the aging process. Few people can live truly independently for the remainder of their lives.

So to reduce the turnover rate and allow seniors to "age in place," many independent living facilities have added a variety of services. Many now include nursing facilities, and some are even building special Alzheimer's units. But take note, most independent living communities accept only ambulatory residents. Depending on the community, residents who later become confined to a wheelchair may be asked to leave or may be allowed to stay if they are able to transfer themselves to and from the wheelchair unaided.

In communities that combine independent living, assisted living, and some level of nursing care, residents using wheelchairs or walkers are usually accepted directly into assisted living or nursing care.

ASSISTED LIVING

Assisted living refers to a custodial level of care for seniors with some functional impairments, either physical or cognitive. At this level seniors receive assistance with one or several activities of daily living (ADLs) such as:

- Eating
- Bathing
- Dressing
- Going to the toilet
- Grooming
- Mobility (walking)
- Transferring (moving to and from bed and chair)
- Medication management (storing, maintaining records of, and reminding patients to take medication)

Assisted living is for seniors who do not need twenty-four-hour nursing care, but who do need some custodial care.

According to The Assisted Living Foundation of America (ALFA) headquartered in Fairfax, Virginia, there are an estimated 30,000 to 40,000 assisted-living facilities in the United States today, housing about one million senior citizens. It is the fastest-growing segment of the senior housing industry.

Residential units in an assisted-living facility are usually rented on a monthly basis. They may be apartments with full kitchens, studios with small efficiency kitchens, or private or semiprivate rooms only. Some facilities do not permit stoves in residential units, either because of safety concerns or state regulations.

Services usually include three meals daily served in a common dining room; assistance with activities of daily living; emergency call systems in each unit; twenty-four-hour security; housekeeping; personal laundry; transportation; and various exercise, recreation, and social programs. General supervision and "cueing" or reminders are also provided for seniors with memory loss.

In some facilities the basic fee covers all services. In others, the basic fee covers only limited services with additional charges for services on an à la carte or as-needed basis.

The number of residents can range from several to several hundred, but assisted-living facilities typically house 25 to 120 residents. A facility may offer just assisted living or may be combined with independent living or nursing care.

Assisted-living facilities are licensed by states under a variety of names. It is important to note these variations so that you will recognize the concept of assisted living even if it is called something else in your community.

Other names for assisted living facilities:

- Residential care facilities
- Personal care homes
- Personal care boarding homes
- Sheltered care facilities
- Adult residential care homes
- Boarding homes
- Basic care facilities
- Enriched housing
- Comprehensive personal care homes
- Adult foster homes
- Supported residential care facilities

See Appendix C for alphabetical listing by state of agencies responsible for regulating assisted living and the term each agency uses to refer to assisted living.

NURSING CARE

The three levels of nursing care provided by nursing facilities are:

1. *Custodial care:* Nonmedical care that includes around-the-clock supervision, as well as assistance with personal needs such as eating, bathing, dressing, grooming, going to the toilet, and mobility.
2. *Intermediate care:* Basic medical care.
3. *Skilled care:* More intensive medical care.

There are two types of nursing facilities associated with residential facilities: *Intermediate care facilities,* which provide custodial and intermediate care, and *skilled-nursing facilities,* which provide custodial, intermediate, and skilled care.

1. *Intermediate-care facility (ICF):* A nursing facility licensed by the state to provide twenty-four-hour basic medical care under the supervision of a registered nurse, who may be on call and not necessarily on duty. Basic medical care includes rehabilitative and recuperative care, but *not* more intensive medical procedures such as intravenous therapy and feeding tubes. The staff-to-patient ratio is lower than in a skilled-nursing facility.
2. *Skilled-nursing facility (SNF):* A nursing facility licensed by the state to provide twenty-four-hour nursing care with at least one registered nurse on duty during the day. Care is provided under the supervision of a licensed physician who is on call. A skilled-nursing facility is equipped to provide more intensive medical procedures such as intravenous therapy and feeding tubes. This is *subacute care,* which is the highest degree of nursing care outside of a hospital.

In order to know what level of care is provided by a facility you need to understand the distinction between the two. When visiting a community that has a nursing unit, be sure to ask if it is a skilled-nursing facility or an intermediate-care facility. Both provide care on a short- or long-term basis, but Medicare will *only* certify facilities that provide skilled-nursing care.

A senior residential facility may provide nursing care on-site or may contract with a nearby facility to provide care to its residents.

How that care is paid for depends on the community and the type of payment plan offered. In a rental community, the rent may include a specified number of days of nursing care. After those days are used up (or if the resident moves into the nursing facility permanently), the resident is charged on a daily or monthly basis. On the other hand, a community that charges an entrance fee may provide unlimited nursing care at no extra charge. However, entrance fee contracts vary. Some entitle the resident to a specified number of days of nursing care and some call for per diem charges for nursing care. (Entrance fees explained on pages 22–24.)

Residential communities with their own nursing facility may accept a limited number of *direct admissions* (residents from outside the facility admitted directly to the nursing unit). Other facilities restrict the use of their nursing units for facility residents only.

The Second Set of Blocks: Methods of Payment

There are three methods of payment at senior residential communities.

1. *Rental*
2. *Purchase* (includes condominiums and cooperatives)
3. *Entrance fee*

Understanding these terms is crucial to your decision-making process. Moving to a residential community is a major financial commitment. Costs vary greatly, but even the least expensive communities are not cheap. It is important to remember, however, that you are paying for more than just shelter. Here money buys a lifestyle, security, companionship, services, and often health care, or at least access to it.

In the discussion of these payment methods, some advantages and disadvantages of each are noted for your consideration.

RENTAL

The simplest and most common form of payment is rental, which is a fixed payment paid by a resident for the occupancy and use of a specified living space. Some facilities require one-year leases, but many rent units on a month-to-month basis.

The rent may include some basic services only (with additional services costing extra), or it may include everything the facility has to offer—meals, transportation, housekeeping, social programs, some health care, and all utilities except telephone.

ADVANTAGES

• *Renting feels less permanent.* It is difficult for most seniors to make the decision (or accept the decision being made for them) to move; it may be easier knowing that they are not permanently stuck in one place. It provides a sense of control over one's life.

• *Renting does not require a large capital outlay.* Many people don't have (or don't want to part with) the cash necessary to buy a condominium or cooperative or to pay an entrance fee.

• *Renting allows flexibility.* If you don't like the place, the management, or your neighbors, you can move. If your daughter, who lives nearby, moves to another city, you can move to be near her.

DISADVANTAGES
•   *Rent increases may prove too much of a financial burden to those on a fixed income.*
•   *Renting does not provide the security of long-term occupancy.* While some people don't like the feeling of permanency, others don't want to face another move. If Dad is ornery and has had several run-ins with the staff, he may be asked to leave. You may love the apartment you are renting month-to-month but are forced by a temporary illness to spend some time in the hospital. At what point can your apartment be rented to someone else? Even though another apartment may be available for you upon your return, you might not like it or its location as much as the first.
•   *Rental communities rarely permit tenants to make substantial changes to units; nor do many tenants want to spend a lot of money fixing up a rental apartment.* On the other hand, condominium or cooperative buyers might want to spend money adding wood floors or enlarging the kitchen to make the residence feel more like the home they left.

PURCHASE
In some communities residents purchase or buy their residential units, which may be apartments, town houses, or detached houses. In such cases, ownership falls into one of two categories: condominium or cooperative.

•   *Condominium:* A form of ownership where a resident has title to his or her residential unit and a shared interest in the common areas of the facility or community. Common areas include those shared by all residents, such as the grounds, hallways, stairs, elevators, parking areas, lobbies, etc. The resident buys his apartment and pays a monthly fee to cover his share of the operating and maintenance costs of the common areas.
•   *Cooperative:* Another form of apartment ownership where the resident, instead of owning an apart-

ment outright, owns shares in a corporation that actually owns the entire building. Those shares allow the resident to *occupy* (not own) a specific unit in the building. A cooperative owner pays a monthly fee to cover his share of the operating and maintenance costs of the building and grounds *plus* his share of the mortgage and taxes for the entire property.

ADVANTAGES
• *Ownership provides a much needed sense of security at a time when everything else seems to be changing.* The American dream of home ownership is rooted so deeply in the psyche that many people who have owned their own home for fifty years or so find the transition to renting difficult. It is bad enough having to scale down from a large house to smaller quarters, but at least it's still home if you own it.
• *Ownership allows residents to make alterations to their units.* Someone who loves to cook and entertain might want to remodel the kitchen. If small rooms make you feel claustrophobic, you can tear down walls and open up spaces. People feel more comfortable living in familiar surroundings.
• *Purchasers who borrow money to buy their condominiums are entitled to income tax deductions on the interest portion of their mortgage payments.* Cooperative owners are entitled to an income tax deduction for the portion of the monthly fee that is applied to the building's mortgage and property taxes.
• *Purchasers don't have to worry about rent increases or losing a lease.*

DISADVANTAGES
• *Ownership hinders one's mobility.* In a few years you may want to move to a different climate or closer to your children, but first you'll have to sell your unit.
• *The condominium association may impose large assessments for a costly maintenance item such as a new roof.*
• *Monthly maintenance fees are not fixed permanently*

and may increase because of inflation or increased operating costs as the property ages.

ENTRANCE FEE, ENDOWMENT FEE, OR FOUNDER'S FEE

In some communities residents sign a contract and pay a lump-sum fee when they enter in addition to a monthly fee. Entrance fee contracts come in a variety of forms. The three elements to consider are

- *Time period:* The contract may be for a specified period or for life.
- *Refundability:* The entrance fee may be refundable, partially refundable, or nonrefundable.
- *Services and health care:* The amount of services and health care included determines whether the contract is one of three types:

1. *Extensive or all-inclusive contract:* The entrance fee includes all services and unlimited health care.
2. *Modified contract:* The entrance fee includes some services and some health care.
3. *Fee-for-service contract:* The entrance fee covers only basic services. Other services and health care are paid for on an as-needed basis.

EXTENSIVE OR ALL-INCLUSIVE CONTRACT

As its name implies, this contract includes everything the community has to offer: shelter, services, amenities, and unlimited nursing care. Extensive contracts have higher entrance fees, but monthly payments remain stable (except for normal increases owing to inflation or increased operating costs). Since this type of contract appeals more to the older, less agile segment of the senior population, facilities that offer *only* an extensive contract will likely house the oldest, sickest, and most frail residents. A healthy seventy-five-year-old may not wish to live here.

MODIFIED CONTRACT

This contract includes shelter, services, amenities, and a limited number of days of nursing care, after which a monthly or per diem rate is charged for nursing care. (Note that some communities charge residents a lower rate for nursing care than they charge to outside patients admitted directly to the nursing facility; others charge a full daily rate.)

FEE-FOR-SERVICE CONTRACT

This plan provides shelter, basic services, and guaranteed *access* to nursing care. The entrance fee and monthly fee are lower than with the extensive or modified plans, but residents pay a full per diem rate for all nursing care. (Some contracts include a few days of nursing care.) Residents pay an additional charge for meals and other services such as housekeeping, transportation, recreational therapy, and other services that are included in the extensive or modified plan. Hence the name fee-for-service. Residents pay only for those services they use.

It is difficult to list advantages and disadvantages of entrance fee contracts because there are so many variables to consider. Is the contract for a limited time or does it cover the resident's lifetime? Is the entrance fee fully refundable, partially refundable, or nonrefundable? If it is refundable or partially refundable, under what circumstances and what timetable? Is the contract extensive, modified, or fee-for-service?

The extensive plan is the most expensive plan initially, but monthly costs remain stable and predictable, regardless of how much nursing care a resident needs over her lifetime. The fee-for-service plan is the least expensive initially, but future costs are unpredictable. Depending on the amount of nursing care and/or services a resident needs in the long run, the fee-for-service plan may turn out to be more expensive.

On the other hand, the fee-for-service contract may represent a considerable savings for residents who remain basically healthy throughout their lives. Then the

Costs for a One-Bedroom Apartment

	EXTENSIVE	MODIFIED	FEE-FOR-SERVICE
Entrance fee	$100,000	$85,000	$40,000
Monthly fee	1,400	1,200	900
Nursing care included	Unlimited	60 days/yr	——
Services included	All utilities except telephone	All utilities except telephone	All utilities except telephone
	Three meals daily	Two meals daily	——
	Prescribed diets	——	——
	Transportation	Transportation	——
	Housekeeping	Housekeeping	——
	Flat linen laundering	——	——
	Exercise programs	Exercise programs	——
	Social programs	Social programs	Social programs
	Emergency call system	Emergency call system	Emergency call system
	Tray service	——	——

question is, why pay an entrance fee at all? Why not choose a rental community with a skilled-nursing facility? The answer may be that you choose to pay an entrance fee because you like the community's location, its ambience, its design, or because you have other friends living there. These are important considerations that may outweigh the financial ones.

In addition to tying up a large sum of money, the most obvious disadvantage to paying an entrance fee is the risk of losing it if the community shuts down. (See Chapter Four, Checking Out the Facility.)

Putting It All Together

Now that we've explained the components—the building blocks—let's see how they might be put together in real life. We'll tour a community called Westlake, which is actually a composite drawn from several existing communities in various parts of the country. To construct Westlake, we've used all three levels of care from the first set of blocks (independent living, assisted living, and nursing care) and only a rental block from the second set. Westlake is a fourteen-story brick structure in the heart of a major city. Notice the myriad amenities, activities, and services, a topic discussed in greater detail in the next chapter.

WESTLAKE

Welcome to Westlake Retirement Center—a rental community offering independent living, assisted living, and skilled-nursing care in a single high-rise building. Residents may enter the community at any level. Units are rented on a monthly basis, with only thirty days notice required for termination.

The first floor contains a marble-tiled reception lobby, large formal living room with a fireplace, restaurant-style dining room, private dining room for entertaining, library, billiard room, auditorium, social lounge, overnight guest suites, arts-and-crafts room, beauty and barber shop, convenience store, and indoor swimming pool. The high-ceilinged common areas, appointed with antique furnishings and decorator fabrics, have an elegant residential feel.

Front door valet service, covered parking, and twenty-four-hour security are provided for the convenience and safety of all residents.

Floors two through ten contain 115 independent-living apartments available in nine different floor plans. The one-, two-, and three-bedroom apartments range in size from 500 to 1,700 square feet. Each has a fully equipped kitchen and some have balconies. Prices range from $1,900 to $3,200 a month and include basic cable television, all utilities (except telephone), continental breakfast and choice of lunch or dinner daily, weekly maid service, weekly linen laundry service, transportation, fifteen days a year of free care in the skilled-nursing center, daily exercise programs, and entertainment and social events.

Residents on the independent living floors must be ambulatory and in good physical and mental health. Equipment such as walkers or portable oxygen tanks is not permitted in the dining room or downstairs lounge and recreation areas. A resident may use a walker to get to the dining room, but must leave it outside in a specially designated area. Residents who are unable to get about unaided must live on the assisted-living floors where separate dining and lounge facilities are provided.

An independent-living resident who becomes ill and is no longer able to meet these requirements must move to assisted living or skilled nursing or move out of the building. If the illness requires only a temporary stay in the nursing center, the resident may return to his apartment. If the resident is out of his apartment longer than sixty days, the apartment may be rented to someone else and another apartment will be provided, based on availability, when the resident is able to return to independent living.

Assisted living is located on floors eleven and twelve. There are forty unfurnished studio apartments that rent for $3,500 a month. Each unit includes a full bath and a kitchenette area with a sink and refrigerator but no stove. All units are equipped with twenty-four-hour emergency call systems.

On the assisted-living floors staff is available to remind residents to take medication, help with personal grooming and hygiene, assist residents to the dining room, or provide help with other daily living activities. In addition to these services, rent includes all utilities (except telephone), basic cable television, twenty-five days a year in the nursing center, three meals a day plus snacks, daily maid service, weekly linen and personal laundry service, exercise programs, transportation, and entertainment and social events.

Each of the two assisted-living floors has its own lounge and dining room where three meals are served daily. Assisted living residents have their own recreational and social programs and may not participate in programs provided for the independent-living residents.

The nursing center on the thirteenth floor contains forty-five private and semiprivate rooms for twenty-four-hour skilled-nursing care on a short-term or long-term basis. These rooms rent on a daily or monthly basis, and the cost depends on the amount of care needed. Ten beds in the nursing center are certified by Medicare for use by eligible residents.

Continuing-Care
Retirement Community (CCRC)

As we've seen, facilities may combine levels of care and methods of payment in a variety of ways and call themselves whatever they like. But there is a particular type of facility called a continuing-care retirement community (often referred to simply as a CCRC) that warrants a separate discussion because of its uniqueness.

There are two defining characteristics of a *continuing-care retirement community*. First, a CCRC provides a continuum of care that includes housing, services, and health care. That does not mean, however, that all three levels of care (independent living, assisted living, and nursing care) are provided. Nursing care is always available, either on- or off-site, but assisted living is not always included.

The second defining characteristic is a contractual agreement between the resident and the CCRC that guarantees these services (or at least access to these services) for a minimum of one year, but usually for the lifetime of the resident. The contract may be set up in a variety of ways. The most common type of CCRC contract is an entrance-fee contract. Whether the contract is an extensive, modified, or fee-for-service type of entrance-fee contract, the resident pays a lump-sum entrance fee plus monthly fees.

Another type of CCRC contract involves an equity agreement where the resident purchases a condominium or cooperative unit instead of paying an entrance fee.

In yet a third, but less common, type of CCRC contract, residents pay monthly fees only.

Continuing-care retirement communities are often confused with the many "look-alikes" that provide a continuum of care but don't have a contract that guarantees services and care for an extended period of time. The Westlake example cited earlier provides all three levels of care and offers residents the opportunity to move from one level to another, but only if and when space is available. Thus Westlake is not a CCRC because there is no contract that provides any guarantees other than a month-to-month lease.

Like many independent living communities, continuing-care retirement communities have been around for years. For the past several decades nonprofit religious or charitable groups have sponsored retirement communities that provide housing, health care, and financial security to residents for the remainder of their lives.

In the past, these were called life-care communities, and residents were usually required to turn over their assets to the community upon entering. Facilities no longer have such a requirement, but the term "life-care community" is still in use. Today, *life-care community* refers to a particular type of CCRC—one that only offers an extensive entrance-fee contract.

Finding Residential Facilities in Your Community

The best way to find a residential facility in your area is to talk to people in the community.

- Friends
- Doctors
- Social workers
- Clergy
- Lawyers
- Accountants
- Librarians

Now that you understand the terms and concepts, you have enough information to begin asking questions. Start by talking to your friends, old and young. Everyone knows someone who has been through the process. Your friend Mary might have a cousin who recently helped find a residential community for her mother-in-law. If you are lucky, she's the kind of person who kept a detailed file of names and phone numbers.

Doctors are another good source of information, particularly those specializing in geriatrics or family practice.

Both social workers and the clergy spend a lot of time dealing with the elderly and may have considerable knowledge about residential communities in the area.

Your lawyer friends involved in estate planning may have consulted elderly clients about residential communities. They might even represent a community or a developer who built one and thus have a lot of information on the topic.

Ask your accountant. Large accounting firms have excellent research departments that can provide a wealth of information.

And don't forget your local librarian who can point you to several sources of information in the public library. The *National Directory of Nursing Homes* found in the reference section is one good example. It lists communities that have nursing facilities as well as free-standing nursing homes.

Following is a list of other places you can call or write for help. It's as easy as dialing a number and asking, "Can you help me find a senior residential facility in my area?"

RESOURCES

American Association of Homes and Services for the Aging
901 E Street, N.W., Suite 500
Washington, DC 20004–2037
202-783–2242
202–783–2255 (fax)

A nonprofit organization that represents the interests of non-profit senior housing facilties. They maintain a national continuing-care database and publish *The Continuing-Care Retirement Community: A Guidebook for Consumers.*

American Association of Retired Persons
601 E Street, N.W.
Washington, DC 20049
202–434–6030
800–424–3410

AARP maintains a limited database of various types of senior housing around the country. They also publish books and pamphlets on housing that may be helpful.

AREA AGENCY ON AGING

There are hundreds of area agencies on aging throughout the U.S. These are federally and state-funded agencies that administer local and regional programs for seniors age sixty and older. Your local area agency can provide you with a list of senior housing facilities in your community.

You can get the number of the agency nearest you by calling Eldercare Locator (800–677–1116) or the National Council on Aging (800–424–9046), both of which are listed below.

Your state unit on aging also can refer you to the area agency nearest you. The numbers and addresses of all 50 state units on aging are listed in Appendix B.

Continuing Care Accreditation Commission
901 E Street, N.W., Suite 500
Washington, DC 20004–2037
202–783–2242

Send a self-addressed, stamped, business-sized envelope for a free list of accredited continuing-care retirement communities.

Eldercare Locator
800–677–1116
(9:00 A.M. to 8:00 P.M. Eastern Standard Time)

National referral service for local sources of information on various topics of interest to seniors, including housing. Call for the name and phone number of agencies in your community that can assist you.

National Association of Geriatric Care Managers
1604 North Country Club Road
Tucson, AZ 85716
520–881–8008
520–325–7925 (fax)

Organization of geriatric-care managers founded in 1986. A geriatric-care manager is a professional (with masters degree and training in gerontology, social work, nursing, or counseling) who specializes in assisting seniors and their families with long-term care.

Call or write for free referral to geriatric-care managers in your area or to order a national referral directory for $35.

National Council on Aging
409 Third Street, S.W.
Washington, DC 20024
202–479–1200
202–479–6674 (TTY)
800–424–9046

Private, nonprofit organization that serves as a national resource for information, training, technical assistance, research, and publications across the spectrum of issues in aging. They can put you in touch with local agencies on aging.

CHAPTER THREE

Visiting Facilities

The previous chapter explained the three levels of care (independent living, assisted living, nursing), the three methods of payment (rental, purchase, entrance fee), and showed how they may be combined in a multitude of ways to form a residential community. Chapter Two also gave some tips on locating such communities in your area. So let's move on to the next step—visiting some of these places.

You probably have a few basic requirements such as location or the need for certain levels of care that will eliminate some facilities from your list. But a word of caution—don't eliminate too many. You may end up choosing the very first place you see, but you'll want to visit others for comparison before making that decision. Each visit will bring new insights about what is available, what is affordable, and what type of facility will best suit your needs. The more information you have, the more secure you'll feel about your decision.

Try to keep an open mind. Don't rule out a place just because it is located in a neighborhood you're unfamiliar with or because a friend didn't like it. Unless you really trust a person's opinion, go see for yourself. How many times have you loved a movie or book that someone else hated? Besides, even if you end up agreeing with your friend, the visit will give you the opportunity to evaluate what you disliked about the facility. That can be as important in your information-gathering process as finding out what you do like.

Consider who will accompany you on these visits. If you are selecting a place for yourself and your spouse, should you weed out a few places before bringing your spouse along? Will he or she be depressed by the process, particularly if you visit some places that you find disagreeable? Or does your spouse need to see the bad to appreciate the good? Only you can answer these questions.

If you are making the decision for yourself alone, should you ask your son or daughter to come along? It is helpful to have emotional support as well as another pair of eyes and ears to observe things you might miss. But is your child too controlling? Will he or she take over and make the decision for you? Maybe it's better to ask your best friend to come along instead.

Similarly, if you are looking for a place for a parent, the optimum situation is to include the parent in the decision-making process as much as possible. But you must take into account his or her temperament and energy level. If your parent is too critical or inflexible, or if the sheer physical energy needed to get in and out of the car and walk around looking at a place would be too exhausting, it may be better to make a few visits on your own first.

So now that you've decided who, if anybody, will accompany you on your visits, you can call and make appointments. Unless time is of the essence, you should schedule only one visit a day. As you will see, there is a lot of information to process, and you may find that all the details run together if you visit several facilities on the same day.

Remember, this is an extremely important decision that should not be taken lightly. Because moving is so emotionally and physically stressful, particularly during the later years of life, most people who make the move to a senior residential facility hope it will be their last move. So the goal is to find the right place—a place that provides an enjoyable lifestyle, companionship, and security, as well as the necessary services and health care.

This takes a lot of thought. Not only must you assess what services and health care you or your parents may need now and in the future, but you should give careful consideration to the less obvious emotional and psychological needs of the person making the move.

Imagine a nature lover whose soul is soothed by trees, flowers, and the sound of chirping birds trapped in an apartment with a view of traffic whizzing by on the freeway. On the other hand, some people feel isolated and depressed staring at trees. Their soul connects with the sights and sounds of city life. Take, for example, the gentleman who worked downtown for fifty years and chose what others thought was a less desirable apartment overlooking the freeway. Sitting at the window watching people commute to and from work energized him.

Or imagine how uncomfortable and out of place a person who spent his life on a farm might feel moving into an elegant high-rise with marble floors and expensive antiques.

So you see, the visit is crucial. A brochure can list the services offered, but you must visit a facility and use all of your senses to determine if it is the right place for you or your family member.

• *Sight:* Look for signs that it is a friendly place. Are employees and residents smiling? Notice telltale signs of neglect—tattered furniture or gardens overgrown with weeds.

• *Sound:* Listen to how the staff speak to residents. Do they call residents by name? Is their tone of voice warm and friendly? Are residents speaking to each other? Do they seem congenial?

• *Touch:* Sit in the furniture. Is it comfortable? Run your hand along the handrails in the hallways. Are they sturdy and placed at a comfortable height? Notice how staff members touch residents. Do they touch the arms or shoulders of residents when speaking in a warm and friendly gesture? Does the touch of staff members seem kind and gentle or rough and impersonal as they help residents move in and out of bed, for example?

• *Smell:* Does the place smell clean and fresh? Strong smells of disinfectant or deodorizer may indicate the staff is masking odors rather than maintaining cleanliness.

• *Taste:* Have a meal. How does the food taste? For many seniors food is the number-one issue in selecting a residential facility.

To help organize your visit, a detailed checklist of things to look for and questions to ask is included at the end of this chapter. You might find it helpful to make several photocopies of the checklist so you can fill out one for each visit. The photocopies can be enlarged for easier reading. You may also find it helpful to give a copy of the checklist to the person accompanying you on the visit. You'll be surprised how many things one of you notices that the other didn't.

At the top is a place for the name and address of the facility, the name and phone number of the person you will meet with, the date and time of the appointment, and space for any notes you might want to make, particularly any distinguishing features that will aid your recall of the place when you get home. If you have a Polaroid, take the camera along on the visit so you can attach snapshots of the facility to your checklist.

The checklist is divided into six sections:

• Overview
• Design features
• Services and amenities
• Levels of care
• Payment
• Other questions to ask

This is a lot of information and not all of it will be relevant to your selection.

The purpose of the checklist is not just to help you gather information, it is also intended to stimulate your thinking about the psychological as well as physical needs of the person making the move. For the move to be successful, it is critically important that you spend some time thinking about the personality, likes and dislikes, and emotional needs of the person moving, whether it is you or someone else.

No place will meet all of anyone's needs, but there are some subtle factors that can make a world of difference between a person being happy or miserable in a new home. For instance, some people don't care about natural light and may actually prefer dark rooms. For others, however, the lack of natural light may cause severe depression. For those people, it is important not only to select a residence with large windows, but to be sure that the glare or heat from the sun on the windows is not so strong that it will be necessary to keep the drapes drawn. Notice whether windows are tinted or double-paned for insulation. Are exposures north or south, or do the windows get the intense morning and afternoon sun of east and west exposures?

Whether you actually fill out the checklist or just use it as a guide of things to look for, a careful reading of this chapter will heighten your awareness of the importance of details and enable you to make a more informed decision.

Overview

This section should be filled out last, but it is placed first to provide a quick summary of important details. Items covered include location (urban, suburban, rural) and the convenience of the location (for access to family, friends, doctors, church, shopping, and bank); physical layout of buildings (high-rise, cluster of attached low-rises, campus setting, etc.); age of the facility and whether it was purpose-built or renovated; levels of care (independent living, assisted living, nursing); method of payment (rent, ownership, entrance fee); and whether the facility has a religious affiliation.

The overview also provides an opportunity to reflect on the overall living environment at that facility. Is the atmosphere positive and cheery? Does the staff seem kind, patient, and well trained? Does the facility provide residents with privacy, independence, safety and security, social interaction, dignity, and respect?

Design Features

This section is divided into two categories:

- Exterior
- Interior

EXTERIOR

The exterior features are the first things you should notice when arriving for your visit, and are important clues in determining whether the community has a residential rather than an institutional feel. Is it a place that looks inviting, comfortable, homey? Wood or brick exteriors feel more residential than concrete or stone surfaces. Multipaned windows, shutters, porches, potted plants and window boxes, gardens, circular drives, and gas lamps are all details that enhance the residential feel of a building.

Careful planning and attention to detail on the part of the developer of a project is usually indicative of the overall philosophy of the community. It doesn't take much to make a place inviting and comfortable, and the failure to do so speaks louder than words.

Look for other exterior design details that help create

an environment that is user-friendly to senior citizens. Are there walking paths and outdoor seating areas? Remember that if you are an active forty-something looking for a place for Mom or Dad, your busy life may not allow time for sitting beneath a lovely shade tree in the garden, soaking up the fresh air, and smelling the roses, but that could well be a joyful pastime for your parents. It may also be the only time they get out of the building on some days. So not only is having an outdoor area important, it should be esthetically pleasing and inviting with comfortable furniture. What's the point of having a beautiful garden or patio if there's no furniture or if the only place to sit is a backless bench or uncomfortable iron chairs that hurt your back?

Don't overlook parking design, which is a critical concern for many seniors who consider their car their lifeline to independence. Is there covered parking? How far from the residential building is the parking area? Is it attached to the residential building by a covered walkway? Is the parking well lighted and secured? Don't forget to notice how wide the parking spaces are. Tight parking spaces in poorly designed garages can be disastrous for senior citizens, who usually feel more comfortable driving large cars and who may not be able to gauge distances as accurately as they once could. Painted raised curbs in parking areas and along drives are also helpful to seniors.

INTERIOR

The services and amenities provided at a facility will be listed in a brochure and pointed out on a visit. Equally important, however, are interior design details that provide for the safety, as well as the physical and psychological comfort, of residents. The staff at a well-designed facility will point out these features, but it will be up to you to notice their absence at other facilties.

The first thing to notice when you walk in the door is whether the overall feel is residential or institutional. Remember that the main reason seniors resist moving to a residential facility is that they associate them with institutional-type nursing homes. Despite the fact that many people move to a facility because of its health-care component, residents want a facility to feel like home.

One of the most important elements in creating a residential environment is the use of space. Large lobbies and dining rooms have the feel of an institution or a commercial establishment such as a hotel. The way to create a homey environment that Mom or Grandma would feel comfortable in is to divide the large space into smaller, cozy spaces, such as a living room with a fireplace, an entrance parlor, and small dining areas.

Consider other elements that help create an environment that is comfortable and pleasing to the elder generation. Artwork as well as furnishings should be traditional, rather than contemporary. While you may be an abstract art enthusiast, your eighty-something parents probably prefer traditional landscapes and representational artwork.

Is the furniture comfortable for seniors? Remember that older, stiffer joints make getting out of low, soft seats difficult. Sofas and chairs should have high seats with firm cushions and arms for support.

Lighting is an extremely important element in designing for seniors. As we age, our eyes receive less light and become more sensitive to glare. At age sixty we need two to three times more light to see well than we need at age thirty. Not only does the aged eye receive less light, but the weakening of muscles that control pupil dilation causes a reduction in the eye's capacity to respond quickly to changes in light levels.

Rooms should be well lit with even lighting to avoid the contrast of bright and shadowed areas. The light source should also be indirect whenever possible to reduce glare. Highly reflective surfaces such as marble, ceramic tile, and polished wood produce glare and should be avoided. Glare from windows should be minimized. Windows that face north or south are preferable to those that face east or west with strong morning and afternoon exposures to the sun.

Colors and patterns are other important considerations. Dark walls and carpeting reflect too little light and make rooms appear gloomy. Boldly patterned carpets (which are confusing to the aged eye) and carpets with bold borders (which the aged eye may perceive as a step) should be avoided. Contrasting colors should be used, however, to help identify specific areas, pathways, and the placement of furniture. A cream-colored chair on a cream-colored rug is difficult to distinguish; whereas a bold-colored chair on the same carpet is readily discernible.

Carpets with a loop pile or densely woven, short cut pile are better than a deep pile for wheelchair maneuverability.

While touring a facility, don't be so distracted talking with your tour guide that you forget to notice the hallways. Not only are narrow, dark hallways depressing and gloomy and feel institutional, but they can be hazardous. Hallways should be well lit, have handrails disguised as ornamental chair rails to enhance the residential feel, and should be wide enough to maneuver wheelchairs and ambulance stretchers in case of emergency.

There are many design features that help make residential units user-friendly for seniors. Wide doors, doors that open out rather than in, lower counters and shelving, lower placement of light switches, higher placement of electrical outlets, and bathroom grab bars are important, not just for residents in wheelchairs but for those with decreased flexibility of movement.

The space itself should be laid out with as few sharp angles as possible. Whether in a wheelchair or not, residents should not to have to negotiate many turns to get from one space to another, particularly the bathroom.

All senior residential facilities should have emergency call systems in each living unit. There should at least be an emergency call button by the bed, but some facilities also include one in the bathroom. Older facilities or those in renovated older buildings may use the telephone as the emergency response system because of the expense of adding the necessary wiring to install pull cords or call buttons.

Check the bathrooms. Do they have tubs, showers, or whirlpools with grab bars and nonskid surfaces? Remember that most seniors have difficulty climbing in and out of tubs and prefer walk-in shower stalls with seats.

Notice other important features such as thermostats with large calibrations for easier reading. Hardware with levers rather than knobs is easier for arthritic hands to operate. Sheet vinyl flooring in baths and kitchens is safer than ceramic tile or marble, which are more slippery when wet and more damaging to brittle bones in case of a fall.

Storage is a major concern for seniors who are downsizing from a larger house or apartment. Are there enough cabinets and closets, and is the space easily accessible? Do closets have lighting? Some facilities provide separate storage units on each floor or in the basement. Are the storage units climate controlled? What about window treatments? Are drapes, shutters, or blinds provided? If so, would you be allowed to change any you don't like? What other types of changes are allowed? Can you paint, install or remove carpeting, change flooring, take down walls to enlarge rooms, or renovate the kitchen?

And don't forget to notice the proximity of the residential units to elevators, common laundry rooms, and the dining hall/restaurant. You don't want Mom or Dad to skip meals because the walk to and from the dining room is too tiresome. Long hallways should have benches or chairs for resting.

Services and Amenities

SERVICES

While some senior residential facilities may provide only basic services, most offer a wide array of services designed to enhance the lifestyle of their residents. It's important to determine, however, which services are included in your monthly cost, which services are not included, and what is the extra cost of those services not included.

Courtesy transportation is usually scheduled at certain times to specific places like nearby grocery stores, banks, and area malls. Can you also arrange transportation to your doctor's office or to other unscheduled locations?

Is housekeeping provided daily, weekly? What exactly will the housekeeper do—laundry, windows, mopping? Some places include personal laundry service, others offer linen service only. Does the residential unit include a washer and dryer, or do residents share facilities in a common laundry room? How conveniently located is the laundry room? Are the machines coin-operated?

Check out the security. Is twenty-four-hour security provided? Is there an alarm system and controlled access gates for perimeter security? Are there individual smoke alarms and sprinklers in each residential unit as well as in the common areas? What is the procedure for monitoring emergency call systems and checking on residents daily? Some facilities have computerized telephone systems that notify the staff if a resident has not placed an outgoing call or answered an incoming call within a twenty-four-hour period.

Some residential facilities offer complimentary moving services to assist residents with their move. The moving service may even include consultation with a decorator who will help residents decide what furniture to bring from their home, how it should be arranged, and what colors, paints, and fabrics to select.

Some facilities also have staff available to fill out medical insurance forms for residents, and some even have a notary public on-site. The staff at some facilities will even do off-site shopping for residents.

Is valet parking offered? Is there a concierge or doorman to assist with packages and groceries? Are there maintenance personnel to call for repairs? Is the newspaper delivered to residents' front doors?

Food service is a critical issue of concern for seniors moving into a residential facility. You should not make a final decision about a place without tasting the food. Ask to have a meal there. Don't be shy. Have lunch and come back for dinner on another day.

Is the food appetizing, and is there enough of a selection that you might want to eat there every day for years? Most facilities realize that seniors prefer traditional fare to rich, gourmet food. Baby boomers may love exotic, fancy cuisine, but remember that Mom and Dad grew up in an era of home-cooked meals of soup, meat loaf, and potatoes. Older people have a more difficult time digesting rich, spicy foods, but that doesn't mean food has to be bland. Request a sampling of menus from previous weeks or months to see if selections vary.

Look for a menu that offers healthy, low-fat, cholesterol-free selections. It's surprising how many don't! And will the restaurant prepare special meals for residents on restricted diets? Is there a licensed dietician on staff?

Pay attention to the service. Is it prompt and friendly? Are meals served family-style at large tables? Is seating assigned or is the service restaurant-style with individual tables? Do the tables have tablecloths, fresh flowers, and candles? Is the food served hot? Are second helpings available?

What are the hours and who can eat in the main dining room? Are wheelchairs and walkers allowed? Is tray service to your room provided in case of illness?

How many, if any, meals are included in your monthly charge? Some places include continental breakfast and either lunch or dinner daily, some include just one meal a day, and others charge extra for the meal plan. Is the charge prorated for meals missed because of vacations or illness?

AMENITIES

More and more residential facilities are including a full range of amenities to make life more convenient and pleasurable for seniors. Most all places offer exercise, recreation, and social programs. Look for the posted sign-up sheets for these activities to get an idea of what the daily programs include, and how many residents actually participate.

Your tour guide will point out the various spaces designated for activities. It is one thing to say in a brochure that an arts-and-crafts program is offered, but is there an arts-and-crafts room? Does it look like a place where residents work on fun projects? Other speciality areas might include a billiard room, a workshop, library, card and game room, music room, exercise room, theater, auditorium, and meeting rooms. Ask about the activities.

Does the facility provide enough opportunity for physical activity? Is there a swimming pool? Is it indoor or outdoor, is it heated, and does it have good stair rails to facilitate getting in and out easily? Are there walking paths, shuffleboard, and areas where residents can garden?

Some facilities even have a golf course and tennis courts, but nonusers may resent sharing the expense of such costly amenities. If you or your parent is a tennis player, notice if the courts are hard or soft surface. Most older players prefer rubico, clay, or other soft surfaces, which are easier on knees and the back. Are the courts lighted for nighttime use?

Check out the exercise equipment. Is it good equipment and are there enough machines? Is there a full-time attendant? Is there a masseuse on staff?

More and more facilities also include conveniences such as a bank, hair salon, dry cleaners, travel agent, postal center, gift shop, pharmacy, and grocery store. Are lounges equipped with cable television and is the reception good? Is there satellite TV?

Does the facility provide guest rooms that residents

can reserve for their overnight guests and a private dining room for entertaining? Are residents' families invited to participate or help with activities? Is there a chapel? Are services of various denominations held?

Levels of Care

Residents moving into facilities that combine different levels of care will want to have a clear understanding of whether the facility segregates residents in each level or whether residents of all levels are mixed together.

Many facilities segregate independent-living residents from those in higher levels of care for morale purposes. Most healthy, active seniors find it depressing to be around others on a daily basis who are mentally or physically incapacitated. Wheelchairs, walkers, oxygen tanks, memory loss, and other signs of aging are all disturbing reminders of what may lie ahead for each of us.

Assisted living residents, however, may have a different view. A resident who is mentally alert and still physically active, despite the use of portable oxygen for a pulmonary problem, might well resent not being able to sit in the dining room or participate in social activities with independent-living residents.

INDEPENDENT LIVING

Whether a facility offers only independent living or combines it with other levels of care, it is important to understand that facility's qualifications for independent living. What are the entrance requirements, including a minimum and maximum age limit? Is a physical examination required and can you go to your personal physician for the exam?

What types of health problems might force you to move out of the facility or to the assisted-living or skilled-nursing level? Who makes that decision? Can you keep your apartment and for how long if you are moved to a higher level of care on a temporary basis?

ASSISTED LIVING

Even if you are moving into the independent-living section of a facility, you should understand what is offered on the assisted-living level in case you need to move there in the future, either permanently or temporarily.

Does the staff provide assistance with a full range of daily living activities or just some? Do some services cost extra? Is a care plan established for each resident? Is staff available twenty-four hours? What services are provided? Can you hire outside help for special services? Are assisted-living units completely segregated from independent-living residents?

Do residents eat in common dining rooms? Are meals provided at set times? Is seating assigned? Can residents request substitutions for foods they dislike? Are snacks provided? Do residential units have kitchens, and, if not, can residents eat or keep food in their units? Do units have private baths and door locks?

The Assisted Living Facilities Association of America suggests you also check the facility's policy regarding storage of medication, assistance with medication, and record keeping. Are residents allowed to keep any medication in their residence and take it on their own? Who coordinates home-care visits from a nurse, physical therapist, or occupational therapist, if needed? Does a physician or nurse visit residents regularly to provide medical checkups? What is the procedure for responding to a resident's medical emergency?

NURSING

Remember from the previous chapter that there are three types of care provided in nursing facilities:

- *Custodial:* Nonmedical care that includes supervision and assistance only.
- *Intermediate:* Basic medical care.
- *Skilled:* More intensive medical care.

Both intermediate and skilled-nursing facilities provide custodial nursing care for people who do not need medical treatment, but who, for whatever reason, are unable to care for themselves. The important distinction in choosing a facility with a nursing unit is whether the nursing unit provides intermediate or skilled care. Remember that only facilities that provide skilled-nursing care can be certified by Medicare. (See Chapter Five, Understanding Medicare, Medicaid, Medigap and Long-Term Care Insurance.)

An intermediate care facility provides twenty-four-hour basic medical care under the supervision of a registered nurse who may be on call and not necessarily on duty. Basic medical care includes rehabilitative and recuperative care, but not more intensive medical procedures such as intravenous therapy and feeding tubes.

A skilled-nursing facility provides the most intensive level of medical care available outside of a hospital. Care is provided twenty-four hours a day by licensed nursing personnel with at least one registered nurse on duty during the day.

A skilled-nursing facility also has a medical director, who is a licensed physician on call and available to the facility twenty-four hours a day. Ask about the medical director's philosophy on end-of-life issues such as pain management and feeding tubes. A director may, for instance, insist on feeding tubes despite the wishes of the patient or the patient's family. How many hours or days each week is the medical director on the premises?

Is the nursing facility located on- or off-site? How many beds does it have? How many beds, if any, are certified by Medicare and/or Medicaid? How much health care is included in the cost of your residential unit? What is the per diem charge should you need more health care?

Are both single- and double-occupancy rooms available? Do shared rooms have privacy curtains and headsets for television? Do rooms have private baths? Are long-term-care residents allowed to bring their own furnishings to personalize their rooms?

Ask what would happen if you need to move temporarily or permanently to the nursing facility and there is no space available? What specific health-care services are included in your cost or offered at extra charge: occupational therapy, psychiatric treatment, dental care, eye exams, speech therapy, intravenous therapy, wound care, and routine physical checkups?

Is the staff equipped to deal with Alzheimer's or memory-disorder patients? Is there a special Alzheimer's unit? Are Alzheimer's patients segregated from other patients? What is the facility's policy on physical restraints?

Are visiting hours restricted? Does the facility accept direct admissions to the nursing level or is the nursing facility reserved only for independent- or assisted-living residents?

When touring the nursing facility, carefully observe the appearance of the residents and the attitude and demeanor of the staff. Are residents sitting up, well-groomed, and dressed in clean clothes? Are the men clean shaven? Has someone taken the time to brush the residents' hair and clean their fingernails?

Take note of how the staff speak to and physically handle residents. Are staff members kind and gentle, enthusiastic and friendly? And, most important, are all residents treated with dignity and respect?

A basic understanding of the terms used to describe nursing facility staff members will be helpful as you tour the facility.

• *Nurse assistant (or aide):* A person who assists residents with personal care (bathing, toileting, dressing) and other nonmedical procedures under the supervision of a registered or licenced practical nurse. Nurse assistants who work in nursing facilities certified by Medicare and Medicaid must be trained, tested, and certified.

• *Licensed Practical Nurse (LPN):* A nurse who is licensed by the state to provide personal care and to administer certain technical procedures to residents under the supervision of a registered nurse. LPNs must complete a one-year nursing program and pass a state licensing exam.

• *Registered Nurse (RN):* A nurse with the highest level of education and licensed by the state to perform the widest range of nursing services.

• *Medical director:* A licensed physician responsible for supervising the nursing care provided in the facility. The medical director may work full time at the facility or may practice elsewhere while being on call or available to the facility.

• *Administrator:* The person responsible for the day-to-day operations of the nursing facility.

• *Private duty nurse:* A registered nurse hired and paid directly by a resident for individual care.

Payment

Whether you are renting, buying, or paying an entrance fee at a facility, you should have a lawyer review any contract before you sign it. The different methods of payment and contracts will be discussed in greater detail in the following chapter, but there are some basic facts you should make note of when first visiting a facility.

First and foremost, what type of facility is it?

• Rental
• Ownership (condominium or cooperative)
• Entrance fee
• A combination of the above

Rental

If it is a rental facility, is it month-to-month rental or are you required to sign a lease? Is the lease for six months, one year, or longer? Can you terminate the lease and under what circumstances? Exactly what services, amenities, and health care are included in the rent?

Ownership

Are you buying a condominium, where you will actually own your residential unit and an undivided interest in the common areas of the facility, or a cooperative, where you will purchase shares in a corporation that holds title to the entire facility and those shares will entitle you to occupy a specific residential unit?

In either case, you will be charged a monthly maintenance fee to cover your share of the cost of maintaining and operating the common areas. How much will that be and what maintenance does that charge cover? Is the fee per person or per couple?

Entrance Fee

If you are signing a contract and paying a lump sum (called an entrance fee, endowment fee, or founder's fee) to enter a facility, there are numerous things to consider. What is the time period of the contract—is it for a specified period of time or for life? Is the fee fully refundable, partially refundable, or nonrefundable?

How much is the fee and what type is it:

- *Extensive (or all-inclusive):* includes all services and unlimited health care.
- *Modified:* includes some services and some health care.
- *Fee-for-service:* includes only basic services; other services and health care are paid for on an as-needed basis.

Other Questions to Ask

Ask for a copy of the residents' handbook so you can look over the rules and regulations. Are pets allowed and what kind? Is smoking permitted in units or common areas? Are residents required to perform any chores? Are there any restrictions on men and women visiting each others' residences? Are there restrictions on overnight guests?

Is the facility for-profit or nonprofit? What is the nonprofit sponsoring organization? If the facility is church sponsored, do most of the residents belong to that religious denomination?

Ask other questions about the resident mix. What is the average age of residents? What is the male-to-female ratio? Where are most of the residents from? If you or your parent are used to living among a more homogeneous population, you should give careful consideration to what type of people live at the facility.

And remember that while you are looking at the facility, the person showing you around is also sizing up you or your parent as a prospective resident. Be assertive and ask questions, but put your best foot forward!

CHECKLIST

FACILITY NAME: _____

ADDRESS: _____

CONTACT PERSON: _____

PHONE NUMBER: _____

APPOINTMENT DATE: _____ TIME: _____

NOTES: _____

_____

_____

OVERVIEW

Location:

_____ urban   _____ rural

_____ suburban

Convenient to:

_____ family   _____ shopping

_____ friends   _____ bank

_____ doctors   _____ church

Physical characteristics:

_____ high-rise   _____ single story

_____ mid-rise   _____ campus

_____ other (_____)

_____ new construction

_____ converted from other use

_____ renovated (when_____)

Levels of care:

_____ independent living   (number of units)_____)

_____ assisted living   (number of units)_____)

_____ skilled nursing   (number of beds)_____)

Payment:

_____ rental (price range _____)

_____ ownership:

_____ condo (price range_____)

_____ cooperative (price range_____)

_____ entrance fee (price range_____)

Miscellaneous:

_____ religious affiliation (_____)

Overall environment:

_____ positive, cheery atmosphere

_____ kind, patient staff

_____ well-trained staff

_____ opportunity for social interaction

_____ safe and secure environment

_____ residents have privacy

_____ residents have sense of independence

_____ residents treated with dignity and respect

DESIGN FEATURES

EXTERIOR

Building Material:

———	wood	———	stone
———	brick	———	concrete
———	marble		
———	other (_____		

Residential details:

——— multipaned windows

——— shutters

——— porches

——— window boxes/potted plants

——— gaslights

——— gardens

——— other (_____)

——— overall residential feel

Outdoor spaces:

———	gardens	———	walking paths
———	greenhouse	———	swimming pool
———	patio	———	whirlpool
———	courtyard	———	tennis courts
———	shaded seating areas	———	shuffleboard
———	trees	———	golf
———	other (_____)		
———	comfortable outdoor furniture		

_____ well maintained

_____ good lighting

Parking:

_____ covered garage

_____ carport

_____ open lot

close to residental building

____way to residential building

)

_____ wide sp

_____ painted curbs

_____ valet service

INTERIOR

Lobby:

_____ residential feel	_____ good lighting
_____ attractively decorated	_____ artwork
_____ comfortable furniture	_____ fireplace
_____ windows	_____ fresh flowers

Floors:

_____ wood	_____ tile
_____ marble	_____ vinyl
_____ stone	
_____ carpet:	

_____ PATTERNED _____ BORDERED

_____ LOOP PILE _____ CUT PILE

Dining areas:

_____ residential feel

_____ attractively decorated

_____ comfortable furniture

_____ windows

_____ good lighting

_____ artwork

_____ fireplace

_____ fresh flowers/other_____

Floors:

_____ wood   _____ tile

_____ marble   _____ vinyl

_____ stone

_____ carpet:

          _____ PATTERNED   _____ BORDERED

          _____ LOOP PILE   _____ CUT PILE

Hallways:

_____ wide   _____ quiet

_____ good lighting _____ benches/chairs

_____ handrails   for resting

Floors:

_____ wood   _____ tile

_____ marble   _____ vinyl

_____ stone

_____ carpet:

          _____ PATTERNED   _____ BORDERED

          _____ LOOP PILE   _____ CUT PILE

Residential units:

_____ entrance hall

_____ living/dining combined

_____ separate dining room

_____ full kitchen

_____ efficiency kitchen

_____ variety of floor plans offered

         ____ NUMBER BEDROOMS ____ NUMBER BATHS

_____ powder room

_____ central air/heat: ____ GAS

         ____ ELECTRIC   ____ INDIVIDUAL THERMOSTATS

_____ ample storage

_____ coat closet

_____ telephone jacks in convenient locations

_____ cable TV

_____ linen closet

_____ built-in bookcases

_____ emergency call button

         ____ BEDROOM ____ BATH ____ OTHER

_____ security alarm

_____ smoke detectors

_____ door locks

_____ individually controlled thermostats

_____ well-designed to maneuver wheelchair/walker

_____ wide doorways

_____ ceiling fans

_____ chandelier

_____ patio/courtyard

_____ balcony/terrace (high, safe railings)

_____ atrium
_____ changes/renovations allowed
_____ close to elevator
_____ close to dining hall/restaurant
_____ afford privacy
_____ quiet

Appliances:

_____ washer/dryer:

   _____ FULL SIZE   _____ GAS

   _____ APARTMENT SIZE   _____ ELECTRIC

_____ refrigerator:

   _____ FULL-SIZE   _____ APARTMENT-SIZE

_____ ice maker
_____ dishwasher
_____ stove:

   _____ GAS   _____ ELECTRIC

_____ built-in oven:

   _____ GAS   _____ SELF-CLEANING

   _____ ELECTRIC

_____ garbage disposal
_____ trash masher

Windows:

_____ large   _____ blinds
_____ good views   _____ shutters
_____ operable   _____ drapes
_____ insulated   _____ sheers
_____ tinted

Floors:

_____ wood (rooms_____)

_____ marble (rooms_____)

_____ stone (rooms_____)

_____ tile (rooms_____)

_____ vinyl (rooms_____)

_____ carpet (rooms_____)

Senior-friendly features:

_____ doors open out

_____ lower counters

_____ lever hardware

_____ light switches placed lower

_____ electrical outlets placed higher

_____ few sharp angles

_____ large-calibrated thermostat

_____ good indirect lighting

_____ lack of reflective surfaces

SERVICES AND AMENITIES

SERVICES

_____ Housekeeping:

_____ daily

_____ weekly

_____ other (_____)

_____ cleaning

_____ personal laundry

_____ linen service

_____ ironing

_____ wash windows

_____ wax floors

_____ transportation

_____ SCHEDULED   _____ CAN ARRANGE

_____ doorman

_____ valet parking

_____ security guard (_____ twenty-four hours)

_____ controlled access perimeter gates

_____ daily monitoring of residents

_____ newspaper delivery to door

_____ maintenance personnel available

_____ moving/decorator assistance

_____ medical insurance billing

_____ notary public

Food service:

_____ restaurant-style dining

_____ buffet service

_____ assigned seating

_____ snacks available

_____ hours of operation (_____)

_____ tablecloths

_____ fresh flowers

_____ good service/friendly staff

_____ provide tray service to residence

_____ prepare special dietary requests

_____ varied selection

_____ nutritional, well-balanced meals

_____ tasty food

_____ fat-free/low-sodium menu items

_____ food served hot

———— second helpings available

———— licensed dietician on staff

———— wheelchairs/walkers permitted in dining
room

Food plan includes:

———— breakfast

  ———— CONTINENTAL ———— FULL

———— lunch

———— dinner

———— snacks

———— credit given for missed meals

AMENITIES

Recreation/entertainment:

———— social programs

———— music room

———— billiards

———— card and game room

———— theater

———— auditorium

———— library

———— meeting rooms

———— overnight guest rooms

———— private dining rooms

———— arts-and-crafts room

———— workshop

———— gardening

———— shuffleboard

_____ good TV reception in lounge area

    ____ CABLE   ____ SATELLITE

_____ chapel

_____ other (_____)

Conveniences:

_____ bank   _____ dry cleaners

_____ grocery   _____ gift shop

_____ pharmacy   _____ travel agent

_____ hair salon   _____ postal center

_____ laundry rooms

    ____ EACH FLOOR   ____ FREE

    ____ CLOSE TO UNIT

_____ other (_____)

Exercise:

_____ exercise room

_____ exercise equipment

_____ classes

_____ masseuse on staff

_____ swimming pool

    ____ INDOOR   ____ EASY IN/OUT

    ____ OUTDOOR   ____ COMFORTABLE LOUNGE

    ____ HEATED   FURNITURE

    ____ LAP LENGTH   ____ CHANGING ROOMS

_____ walking/jogging trails

_____ tennis courts (how many _____?)

    ____ INDOOR   ____ SOFT COURTS

    ____ OUTDOOR   ____ HARD COURTS

_____ golf

    ____ ON-SITE   ____ PRIVILEGES NEARBY

_____ other (_____)

LEVELS OF CARE

Independent living:
   Number of units_____
   _____ minimum age limit (_____)
   _____ maximum age limit (_____)
   _____ must be ambulatory to enter
   _____ must be ambulatory to remain
   _____ residents segregated from other levels of care

Assisted living:
   Number of units _____
   _____ twenty-four-hour supervision
   _____ staff certified
   _____ good staff to patient ratio (_____ patients
        _____ staff members)
           _____ residents segregated from
        independent-living residents
   _____ units include full kitchens or
        _____ kitchenettes
   _____ residents not allowed to eat in units
   _____ residents eat in common dining room
        _____ BREAKFAST   _____ SET HOURS
        _____ LUNCH   _____ ASSIGNED SEATING
        _____ DINNER   _____ TABLE SERVICE
        _____ SNACKS PROVIDED   _____ BUFFET SERVICE
   _____ private baths

_____ door locks

_____ furnished

_____ partially furnished

_____ unfurnished

Services provided:

    _____ assistance with bathing, going to the toilet

    _____ assistance getting in and out of bed

    _____ assistance with dressing

    _____ assistance with eating

    _____ assistance with walking

    _____ medication management

_____ assistance provided as needed

_____ assistance provided on schedule

_____ residents allowed to keep medication in units

_____ hiring of outside help permitted

_____ regular in-house physical checkups by nurse or physician

Skilled Nursing:

Number of units:

    _____ BEDS   _____ PRIVATE ROOMS

    _____ SEMIPRIVATE ROOMS

_____ intermediate care

_____ on-site

_____ off-site

_____ certified by Medicare (Number of beds_____)

_____ certified by Medicaid (Number of beds_____)

_____ private baths

———— personal furnishings permitted

Services included:

———— occupational therapy

———— psychiatric treatment

———— dental care

———— eye exams

———— speech therapy

———— IV therapy

———— wound care

———— routine physical checkups

———— use physical restraints (———— family permission required)

———— restricted visiting hours (————————)

———— individually controlled thermostats

———— large windows (———— good views)

———— direct admissions accepted (how many————?)

———— equipped to deal with Alzheimer's patients

———— Alzheimer's patients segregated

PAYMENT

_____ *Rental*

_____ month-to-month

_____ lease (How long _____?)

What services and health care are included?

_____

_____

_____

_____ *Ownership*

_____ condominium

_____ cooperative

Range of monthly maintenance fees _____

What services and health care are included:

_____

_____

_____

_____ *Entrance fee*

_____ extensive   _____ partially refundable

_____ modified   _____ fully refundable

_____ fee-for-service   _____ contract for life

_____ nonrefundable

_____ contract for specified amount of time (_____)

OTHER QUESTIONS

Rules and regulations:

_____ pets allowed (What kind _____?)

_____ smoking permitted (Where _____?)

_____ alcohol served in common areas

_____ residents required to perform chores

_____ overnight guest restrictions

_____ roommates restricted to spouse or same-sex sibling

_____ dress code in dining areas

_____ unrestricted visiting hours

Resident mix:

_____

_____

_____

_____

_____

_____

_____

CHAPTER FOUR

Checking Out the Facility

Chapter Three outlined in detail things to look for and questions to ask when visiting facilities. With that information you should be able to narrow down your choices to one or two places that you feel will be the best fit for you or your family member. You've done a lot of work, but you're not finished yet! The next step—checking out the facility—is an essential part of the process.

A facility may be well-designed, beautifully furnished, and provide all the services you're looking for, but if it goes bankrupt five months after you move in, you'll be worse off than when you started. The worst case scenario is obvious. If you paid a $40,000 entrance fee to a facility that goes out of business, whether it's five months or five years down the road, not only do you have to find another place to live, but you also lose your $40,000.

There are other financial losses if a facility goes out of business. The numerous expenses associated with moving to a new home add up quickly. Even if you're renting, if you've just paid a moving company to move your furnishings, paid for custom-made drapes or new window blinds, installed several light fixtures, and the facility then closes, you're still out a chunk of change.

But as bad as the financial loss may be, that's only part of the problem. Any move—particularly for the elderly—is physically and emotionally draining. Imagine that Dad has finally made the decision to move. You have spent months helping him find a place, sell his house, move his things, fix up his new apartment, and now a year later just when he's settling in and making friends, he has to start all over again.

Even if a financially troubled facility doesn't actually close, Dad may find himself stuck in a place where the quality of life and quality of care has declined. It's a sure bet that a facility with money problems will reduce services, personnel, or maintenance to cut costs.

Maybe money is not the root of the problem at a facility. Lack of experience and poor management can also cause the quality of care to suffer. Then what? Should Dad move to another facility or settle for less than expected? Maybe the facility forces Dad out because of certain health requirements or rules and regulations that he didn't really understand beforehand. Maybe he has to move because monthly fees have increased far beyond what is affordable on his fixed income.

Such unhappy situations can be avoided by taking the time to investigate a facility before moving in. Don't rush into a decision based on slick brochures and enthusiastic marketing personnel. Ask questions, read the fine print, check references, and seek the professional advice of lawyers and financial advisers.

If you hire a consultant to help you find the right residential facility, check out the consultant's reputation first. Make sure that the person you are paying for advice is not also receiving a commission or finder's fee from any facility. Obviously, if a consultant recommends a facility that is paying him or her for placing residents there, then the consultant does not have the residents' best interest at heart. Ask a consultant if he or she has a financial arrangement with any facilities. The consultant should be willing to sign a simple statement to that effect. Also ask a facility recommended by a consultant whether there is any financial arrangement between the two.

Your goal is to find out as much as you can about the facility and the people behind it before making a commitment. What is the facility's current financial condition and past financial history? How long has the facility been in operation? What is the experience and background of the owners and management company? Does the facility have the necessary license and/or certification to operate? What kind of experience and training does the staff have? What is the staff-to-resident ratio? What is the turnover rate of residents and why have residents moved? What has been the turnover rate of administrative personnel? These are just some of the questions you need to ask.

Your research should focus on five major areas of concern:

1. Background and experience of developer/owner/manager/sponsor
2. Financial condition of facility
3. License/accreditation
4. Contract
5. References

Background and Experience of Developer/Owner/Manager/Sponsor

Remember that a facility is only as good as the people behind it. The first thing you want to check out is the reputation, experience, and background of the people who developed, own, manage, and sponsor the facility. That may be one person or company or four separate entities, and it is important to understand the difference.

The *developer* is the person or company responsible for taking a project from conception through completion. That includes getting the project designed, financed, and built. Some developers are paid a fee to develop a project for someone else, the *owner*. Once the project is complete, the developer is out of the picture and moves on to develop another project. Many developers, however, build a project to keep, so they are also the owners. In either case, the owner then manages the property or hires a *manager* to oversee its day-to-day operation.

Residential facilities are either owned for profit (also called *proprietary*) or not-for-profit. A nonprofit facility has a *sponsor*, which is a corporation, partnership, or association that has tax-exempt status. Churches, civic associations, or fraternal orders are typical sponsors. The sponsor's association with the facility not only gives the facility its nonprofit status but also provides a degree of credibility. The sponsor may or may not have some financial or legal obligation to the facility.

DEVELOPER

If you're looking at an older, established facility, you need not be particularly concerned with who developed it. But if you're considering a new facility, the experience and background of the developer is important.

The number-one question to ask is whether or not the developer has experience with retirement facilities, and, if so, how many facilities, what types, and how many total residential units are included? For example, if you're looking at a 200-unit continuing-care retirement facility, you would want to know if the developer's only previous experience was developing a 20-unit assisted-living residence.

One of the primary reasons that a number of senior residential facilities failed in the past is that they were developed by people new to the industry. A rash of overbuilding in the hotel, office, and apartment markets in the 1980s left a lot of developers looking for different types of projects to build. Enticed by the demographics of our aging population, a number of developers rushed into the rapidly growing senior housing industry. What many failed to realize, though, is that a senior residential facility is not a real estate project but rather a service-intensive business where management is the key. It's not enough to choose a good location and put up a well-designed building; developers of senior residential facilities must have a clear understanding of the needs and wants of the elderly.

That doesn't mean that a developer new to the industry cannot develop a good project. But if a developer does not have a track record, you should pay close attention to the details of the facility.

OWNER

If the developer does not own the facility, who does? Was the facility developed for the owner or did the present owner buy it from a previous owner? If so, find out when and why the previous owner sold the property.

It may be that the current owner acquired the facility through bankruptcy proceedings. Ask about the circumstances, but understand that a bankruptcy is not necessarily bad for consumers. Suppose a facility was well-conceived but ended up in bankruptcy because the owner spent too much on the design and construction of a building with many luxurious details, and then couldn't fill up the place because of exorbitant rents needed to pay off the debt. Then the owner defaults on the loan and the bank takes back the project, usually reselling it at a much lower price to someone else. Because the new owner paid much less for the project, he can charge more reasonable rents that will attract new residents. In that case, the losers are the bankrupt owner and probably the bank, but the residents end up with a higher quality building than they might have been able to afford otherwise.

On the other hand, if the project went bankrupt because it was built in a bad location, is poorly designed, or is shoddily built, there's not much a new owner can do to make it successful.

Find out as much as you can about the owner. What is the owner's experience with senior housing? Don't settle for how many years the company has been in business. It's quite possible that until recently the company has been in the business of owning apartment buildings or something else not related to senior residential facilities.

The information you want is the number and type of facilities owned and the total number of residential units in those facilities. Does the owner usually retain ownership or sell? Is the owner a privately held company, which may limit your access to financial information, or a publicly held company where financial records are more accessible to the public? These are questions you need to ask, and any reputable facility will readily provide the answers.

MANAGER

Who manages the facility? Whether the owner manages the facility or contracts with a management company, the amount of experience the manager has with senior housing is vitally important. Remember that the number of years in the business is not the most important element, particularly since this is a relatively new industry. The total number of facilities and number of units managed is the key factor. A company that has only been in business for three years, for instance, but manages eight facilities with 1,100 units might be considered experienced.

It is also important to know how long the manager has been at this facility. If the management is new, ask about the previous management. How long was the previous management at the facility? A high management turnover is a red flag, and you need to find out what problems have caused this to happen. Management is crucial to both the quality of care and the happiness of residents.

A high turnover rate among residents is another sign of potential management problems. What is the average length of time residents stay at the facility and what are their reasons for leaving? This information is particularly pertinent in facilities with different levels of care. Most residents who move to facilities that provide a continuum of care do so with the notion that they will remain there for life. If a high percentage of residents move out, rather than transferring to a different level of care, there is a problem.

On the other hand, a facility that is strictly assisted living will typically lose residents as some become too frail to remain and others improve enough to live independently or with family members again.

Ask what the occupancy rate at the facility is. The management at a facility that is 100 percent occupied and has a waiting list must be doing something right. Likewise, a facility that is only 70 percent occupied may have a management or other type of problem, and you need to take a close look at the situation. Remember that a new facility will take a while to fill up, but a good one should be about 80 percent occupied within two years.

SPONSOR

Most people assume that a sponsoring organization is legally and/or financially responsible for the facility it sponsors. The assumption is that you need not worry about your future at the facility, because if the facility runs into financial trouble, the sponsor will bail it out. That is not necessarily true.

A sponsor may actually build and own a facility, in which case the sponsor does remain financially and legally responsible for it. Many sponsors, however, form a separate nonprofit subsidiary to develop and own the facility in order to protect the sponsor's assets from liability. Or, as is often the case, a sponsor may lend its name and reputation to the facility without having any financial or legal responsibility to it. Most sponsors claim, however, a moral obligation to the facility, and many residents feel secure with that commitment.

So check out the sponsor. What is the sponsor's legal and financial relationship to the facility? How involved with policy making is the sponsor? Does the sponsor have experience with other facilities? Ask for a list of the sponsor's board of directors or trustees. What is the reputation of those individuals in the community? The type of people an organization asks to serve on its board tells you a lot about the organization itself.

Financial

Having checked out the people behind the facility, you now need to look at the numbers. Does the facility have the financial strength to remain in operation and to continue to provide the services it promises?

You should ask questions and gather information, but depending on your expertise you may need to seek the advice of professionals such as bankers or accountants to help you interpret the facts.

There are four things you should ask the facility for:

1. Financial statement
2. Operating budget
3. Credit references
4. Information about liens and lawsuits

FINANCIAL STATEMENT

A *financial statement* is simply a report containing financial information about a company. It includes a balance sheet and an income statement.

- *Balance sheet:* Lists the company's assets and liabilities during at a stated point in time.
- *Income statement:* Lists the company's revenues,

expenses, and resulting profits or losses over a stated period of time.

Ask for a copy of the facility's most recent audited financial statement, but take note that not all facilities have audited statements. Publicly held companies listed on a stock exchange are required by the Securities and Exchange Commission to provide audited financial statements so that people buying stock in those companies can rely on the financial information included. Since privately held companies are not regulated by the Securities and Exchange Commission (SEC), most do not incur the added expense of having audited statements unless required to do so by their lender.

Just what does "audited" mean? *Audited* means that the statement has been prepared by a certified public accountant (CPA) and that the CPA has verified the accuracy of the data in the statement. There are two types of audited statements: unqualified and qualified.

• *Unqualified:* Means the statement has been prepared according to the strict requirements of Generally Accepted Accounting Principles (GAAP) adopted by the Financial Accounting Standards Board and the American Institute of Certified Public Accountants. The CPA certifies that the information in the statement is fairly and accurately represented.
• *Qualified:* Means there are some exceptions or things that don't conform to GAAP requirements. All exceptions are explained in the statement. A qualified statement is not necessarily bad; it depends on what the exceptions are.

Just because a financial statement was prepared by a CPA does not mean it is audited. CPAs also prepare unaudited statements, usually called *compilations*. With compilations the CPA collects and assembles—or compiles—the data provided by the client, but does not verify the accuracy of that information. For example, a client might tell his CPA that he spent $5,000 on office equipment, but the CPA does not examine the client's books to verify that information.

This may be more than you care to know about financial statements, but you should understand the basics. What you are looking for when you ask a facility for a financial statement is evidence of that facility's financial viability. You may feel more comfortable making that evaluation based on an unqualified audited statement, but you should not be scared away from a facility with either a qualified or an unaudited statement. Let your financial adviser determine the bottom line.

In addition to requesting the financial statement of the facility, you may wish to look at the financial statement of the facility's owner. This is particularly advisable if the facility is owned by a start-up company without a track record or if the facility itself is new.

Since most new facilities operate at a loss initially, you want to know if the company that owns it has enough cash flow to cover these losses during the start-up period. Ask how many other new facilities the company owns or is planning in the immediate future. Does the company have enough cash flow to cover several start-up operations, or is the company spreading its financial resources too thin?

A financial statement will also help you determine whether a facility that charges an entrance fee and promises to provide future health care has a reserve account sufficient to cover those costs. Whether you sign an extensive contract that covers all future health care or a modified contract that covers some future health care, you want to be sure that the facility has set aside enough money to deliver on that promise. It should also have a reserve account sufficient to pay back refundable entrance fees.

OPERATING BUDGET
An operating budget is a another helpful tool in evaluating a facility. A financial statement is a snapshot of

the facility's past financial performance during a stated time period, while an *Operating Budget* lists the facility's anticipated income and expenses for a stated time period. The budget will tell you what the facility plans to spend money on and where that money will come from. A look at capital expenses will tell you how much money the facility plans to spend improving, rather than just maintaining, the property.

The budget will also reveal any planned cuts. If, for example, the financial statement reveals that the facility has operated at a deficit for the past two years, the budget will show where cuts will be made to cover those losses. Be aware that staff and services are likely to be the first items cut.

CREDIT REFERENCES

Most facilities will provide credit references only when asked, but even then it may be difficult to get much useful information from these references. Bankers, for instance, are prohibited by confidentiality rules from revealing information without the written consent of the debtor. But if the facility refuses to authorize the release of credit information, you should wonder why.

LIENS AND LAWSUITS

Any liens or lawsuits filed against the facility, the owners, or the managers could have significant impact on the financial stability of the facility.

A *lien* is a legal claim on someone else's property as security for an unpaid debt. That means that the debt may be collected by foreclosing on the property. A mortgage is a lien, but it is one that is expected in most cases. What is not expected is a lien filed by a creditor who has not been paid. Typically, this would include money owed suppliers or laborers. If, for instance, the facility has not paid the plumber for work done or the linen supplier for linens delivered, that person may have filed a lien against the property. If the debt is not paid, the property can be sold at foreclosure and the proceeds used to pay off the debt.

To find out if there are any liens against the facility, check with the local tax office or property office. If the facility owes a roofer $1,000, it is unlikely that the property would actually be foreclosed on to pay that debt, although you might question why a relatively small bill has not been paid. But what if the roofer is owed $200,000?

A lawsuit can affect the property in much the same manner. Suppose the family of a resident who dies at a facility sues the facility and its owners for negligence and wins a judgment of $1 million. That judgment can be converted into a lien and is enforceable through a sale of the property.

Financial statements should list any liens or lawsuits against the facility or its owners as actual or contingent liabilities. A lawsuit against management, however, would not be listed in the financial statement because such a lawsuit does not affect the financial condition of the facility. But since management is a crucial component of a successful facility, you should find out the details of any suit filed.

While the facility should be forthcoming with information on liens and lawsuits, you or your lawyer can easily check the public records for this information. Lawsuits can be checked at the local courthouse by simply giving the clerk the names of the facility, its owners, and the management company and asking whether there are any outstanding suits against them. If so, you can obtain a copy of the suit for a nominal fee.

It's important to remember, though, that just because a company has been sued does not mean it has done anything wrong. Find out what the facts are before making a judgment. Also remember that the defendant in a lawsuit may be covered by adequate insurance, in which case the lawsuit would not affect the financial viability of the facility.

Do not be intimidated when seeking information

about a facility. Make an appointment with the facility administrator and ask for the information you want. Be extremely wary of any facility that refuses to cooperate.

In most states Continuing-Care Retirement Communities that charge an entrance fee are required by state law to provide full financial disclosure to residents, as well as to the public. The disclosure documents are reviewed by a state regulating agency, but only to make sure the facility is disclosing the information correctly, *not* to make any determination of the financial viability of the facility.

License / Certification / Accreditation

The next step in checking out a facility is making sure that it has the appropriate credentials. This can be somewhat confusing because different states have different requirements.

First, let's define the terms. A *license* is issued by a governmental agency granting the facility permission to operate. The license indicates that the facility has complied with certain standards and requirements set forth by that agency. Because a license and a certificate are basically the same thing, some states use the term *certified*. However, *certification* more commonly refers to Medicare's approval of a nursing facility. *Accreditation* is a stamp of approval or recognition given by a private organization and does not necessarily indicate fulfillment of legal requirements necessary to operate under state law.

LICENSE
Independent living facilities don't require any type of license to operate, though they must comply with specific building and life safety codes that relate to the design, construction, and safety features of the building.

Assisted-living facilities are licensed by states under

a variety of different names. (See Appendix B for an alphabetical listing by state of the agencies responsible for regulation and how each agency refers to assisted living.) The licensing agency is either the Department of Health or the Department of Social Services. In some states an assisted-living facility need not be licensed if it contracts with an outside company to provide personal-care services.

All *nursing* facilities, whether or not they participate in Medicare and/or Medicaid programs, must be licensed by the state in which they operate. Those that do participate in Medicare and/or Medicaid programs are also governed by federal law.

Continuing-care retirement communities may have several licenses. The nursing facility must be licensed by the state. Communities that have assisted living need a separate license for that level of care. In addition, most states license CCRCs as an entity. That license, usually issued by the state board of insurance, deals with the financial responsibility of the facility. Some states that license CCRCs exclude those that do not charge an entrance fee.

It is best to ask at each facility what licenses are required and whether the facility is licensed and by whom. Ask to see inspection reports, which will list any problem areas. A look at reports for the past several years will tell you if the facility has a history of problems in certain areas and whether the facility is responsible about remedying them.

CERTIFICATION

As of now assisted living is not covered by Medicare in any state and is covered by Medicaid in only a few states, but the assisted-living industry is pushing for change. The industry's argument is that the lack of Medicare and Medicaid coverage forces many elderly residents into nursing homes when their needs would be better served and at less cost by assisted living.

Nursing facilities in all states may choose to participate in Medicare and/or Medicaid programs. Those that do must be certified, which requires compliance with Medicare's stringent "conditions of participation." (See Chapter Five for an explanation of Medicare and Medicaid.)

Because of the high cost of meeting Medicare's rigorous standards, some facilities choose to have only a portion of the facility certified. For example, a fifty-bed nursing facility may have only fifteen certified beds. Some nursing facilities choose not to be certified because they do not want to accept the lower Medicare/Medicaid payments, nor do they want the red-tape hassle. Other facilities simply choose to provide a less intensive level of care than Medicare requires.

So when considering a facility with nursing care ask questions. Is it a Medicare- and/or Medicaid-certified facility? How many beds are certified? If it's not certified, why not? It may be by choice or the failure to meet Medicare and Medicaid standards.

ACCREDITATION

To date there is no accreditation process for independent living, assisted living, or nursing facilities. Only continuing-care retirement communities receive accreditation.

In 1985, the American Association of Homes and Services for the Aging (AAHSA), the trade organization for nonprofit providers of health-care services for the aging, formed an independent commission for the purpose of establishing standards for continuing-care retirement communities. The Continuing-Care Accreditation Commission evaluates both nonprofit and for-profit CCRCs. Those facilities that meet the commission's requirements receive the commission's seal of approval in the form of accreditation.

Because of the commission's high standards, a few states accept accreditation in lieu of state regulation. In Florida, for example, nonaccredited CCRCs have to submit financial reports to the state several times during the year, while accredited facilities do not. The commission is working to expand its acceptance by state regulating agencies.

The accreditation process includes extensive self-study by the facility's staff, board of directors, and residents, as well as an on-site inspection by professionals in the continuing-care industry. All of that information is presented to the national commission in Washington for final approval.

If a continuing-care retirement community is not accredited, ask why. Has the facility been denied accreditation? It may be that the facility is too new; facilities must be 90 percent occupied for at least one year before applying for accreditation.

To obtain a free listing of currently accredited facilities, send a self-addressed stamped envelope to Continuing-Care Accreditation Commission, 901 E Street, N.W., Suite 500, Washington, DC 20004–2037.

Contract

Whether you are renting, buying, or paying an entrance fee, you will sign a contract spelling out in detail the agreement between you and the facility. Whether it's called a *residency agreement, occupancy agreement,* a *residence and care agreement,* or anything else, it is still a legal contract and should be reviewed by a lawyer. Any reputable facility will not only allow but encourage you to take the contract home so you can obtain legal advice. Under no circumstances should you be pressured to sign anything on the spot. Any attempt to pressure you or the refusal to allow you to take the contract with you should be warning enough to look elsewhere.

Consumer laws vary from state to state, but most states have rescission laws that give consumers a specified time (typically varying from three to ninety days) to revoke or cancel certain contractual agreements. A lease, however, is not one of the contractual agreements that can be rescinded. Be sure you understand what your state law provides before signing.

Remember that the contract was written by lawyers who represent the facility and that the contract will be worded in a way that presents the facility in the best light. The Elder Law Practice Guide Series, *Advising Your Client on Continuing Care Retirement Communities,* points out three marketing techniques found in most CCRC contracts*:

- Attractive features are placed at the beginning of the contract and problematic items are placed at the end.
- Euphemistic terms are used to deal with difficult subjects such as death.
- Positive phrases are substituted for negative ones (for example, "No smoking in residential units" becomes "Smoking permitted in designated areas only").

Of course, these techniques are not limited to CCRC contracts, and you should look for them when signing any contract.

Rather than discuss the various types of contracts that you might find yourself dealing with, we will discuss some of the important elements that you should look for in any contract:

- Time frames (duration)
- Fees
- What those fees do and do not cover
- How fees may be increased or decreased
- Refunds
- Termination

*Susan Gorn, *Advising Your Client on Continuing-Care Retirement Communities,* Elder Law Practice Guide Series (Horsham, PA: LPR Publications, 1995), p. 13.

- Insurance
- Changes permitted to living unit
- Rules and regulations
- Transfer to other levels of care
- Nonperformance of facility

TIME FRAMES (DURATION)

How long is the contract for and what are the terms for renewal?

FEES

How much money will you be paying on a one-time basis (in the case of an entrance fee) and on a monthly basis? When is the payment due? Is there a grace period before penalties are assessed for late payment? What are the penalties?

What happens in the event you become unable to pay all or part of your monthly fees? Some facilities will provide financial assistance to residents who are experiencing financial difficulty, although they rarely advertise that fact. Other facilities consider nonpayment just cause for eviction, and some will look to relatives for payment.

WHAT FEES DO AND DO NOT COVER

Specifically, what do the fees cover? Whether you are paying monthly rental or an entrance fee plus monthly fees, your costs will entitle you to a residential unit and some services. Health care may or may not be included.

The residential unit may be a cottage, an apartment, or a private or semiprivate room. Is the specific unit you will occupy designated in the contract, or are you just paying for the right to reside at the facility? Is the residential unit furnished or unfurnished and are appliances included? Be sure the contract spells out which appliances so you don't find yourself having to pay additional money when you move in. Are utilities included (electricity, gas, water, local telephone, basic cable)?

What services are included? Remember that you could rent a comparable apartment for a lot less, but that you are paying a premium for the many services offered at senior residential facilities. Some are included in your monthly cost, and some are available to you at additional cost. The contract may be worded ambiguously so that you believe you are paying for a service, when in fact that service is simply available. Available at what cost and by whom? Does the facility or an outside contractor provide that service? Be sure you understand at the outset which services cost extra and how much extra so that you can calculate your monthly costs accurately.

It is also important to have a clear understanding of what each service entails. Does scheduled transportation mean a van goes to a certain grocery store at specific times on specific days, or can you arrange transportation to your doctor's office as needed? What does weekly housekeeping service mean? Does a housekeeper spend one hour a week dusting your apartment or will the housekeeper mop the floors and clean the bathrooms?

Are you paying for a certain amount of health care or just *access* to health care? Exactly what health-care services are included (skilled-nursing care, eye care, dental care, physical therapy, occupational therapy, speech therapy, routine physical checkups, podiatry, cost of prescription drugs)? Is the facility equipped to deal with Alzheimer's or other cognitive disorders? What is the additional cost of anything not included?

Are those health-care services provided on-site or does the facility contract with a health-care facility off-site? What happens if you need to move permanently or temporarily to assisted living or the nursing facility and there is no space? Does the facility guarantee to locate you somewhere else until space becomes available?

In the case of assisted-living care, exactly what services are provided? Assistance with activities of daily living (ADLs) such as bathing, going to the toilet, ambulation, transfer, eating, grooming, and medication management are usually included. What about assistance with other kinds of activities such as letter writing, check writing, and making phone calls—are they included, too? You should also understand *when* such assistance is available. Is an aide scheduled to help you at a set time each day, or is assistance provided whenever needed?

FEE INCREASES/DECREASES

Under what conditions can your monthly payments be increased? Are there scheduled increases? How often? How much notice will be given residents of impending increases? Are those increases tied to any type of index, such as the cost-of-living index? Is there a cap or limit on how much the costs can be increased over a certain period of time? What about other costs, such as assessments for maintenance and repair items in the case of condominium or cooperative ownership? Ask to see a history of fee increases.

While you don't want to find yourself having to move because monthly costs have escalated beyond the means of your fixed income, you should be wary of a facility that promises *not* to increase fees. How will that facility cover rising costs without letting maintenance and service deteriorate?

How are your costs affected if your spouse moves to a nursing home or dies? What if you divorce or remarry? Does the facility give credit or prorate costs if you take an extended vacation or spend time in the hospital?

TERMINATION

Under what circumstances can either you or the facility terminate the contract? Most contracts state that the facility can terminate for "just cause." You need to ask exactly what is meant by that. How much notice is required for termination? Do you have the right to appeal?

REFUNDS

Refundability is a key issue of concern with entrance-fee contracts. Entrance fees may be fully refundable, nonrefundable or partially refundable, and the contract should clearly state the terms.

What does fully refundable mean? Is that 100 percent of your deposit, or are some costs deducted?

Partial refunds are usually one of two types:

- *Flat-percentage refund:* A flat percentage of the entrance fee is paid if the resident leaves the facility during a specified period of time. For example, a contract might state that 80 percent of the refund is paid if the resident leaves during the first year, 70 percent if the resident leaves during the second year, and 50 percent from years three through five, with no refund paid after the fifth year.
- *Declining-balance refund:* The refund is calculated on a declining scale, subtracting perhaps 1 or 2 percent for each month the resident stays at the facility. There may or may not be a floor or minimum refund paid whenever the resident leaves.

Whatever the type of refund, full or partial, there are several critical questions:

1. What are the circumstances under which the refund will be paid? Is all or part of the entrance fee refundable in the case of:

   - Death
   - Voluntary move (You don't like the facility.)
   - Involuntary move (You're evicted for violating rules, or you require health care not available at the facility.)

2. Is interest paid on the refund?
3. Once the resident leaves, will the refund be paid within a specified time whether or not the resident's unit has been resold or released?
4. Is the refund applicable regardless of which level of care the resident is residing in when he or she dies or moves?

In addition to entrance-fee deposits, there are other refundable deposits that you need to consider:

• Security deposit
• Construction deposit
• Waiting list deposit

Most people are familiar with a *security deposit* that is paid in advance to ensure against any damage (*not* normal wear and tear) to the residential unit. In the event there is no damage, the deposit should be 100 percent refunded within a specified period of time.

A *construction deposit* is paid to reserve a space in a facility that is under construction. If the facility is one that charges an entrance fee, the deposit will typically be 10 to 20 percent of the entrance fee. Ask how many units must be leased or sold before construction can begin (usually a requirement of the lender), and how many units currently are leased or sold. When is completion expected? What happens if the facility is not completed within a certain time? Is your deposit refunded (all or part, with or without interest) if you change your mind, die, or become ineligible before construction is completed? Within what amount of time will that refund by issued?

Many facilities that are full require a *waiting list deposit* (also called a *preoccupancy reservation deposit*) to have your name put on a waiting list. Ask how long the waiting list is. Is your deposit refunded (all or part, with or without interest) if you change your mind, die, or become ineligible? Within what amount of time will that refund be issued?

INSURANCE

Does your monthly cost include homeowner's or renter's insurance to cover your residential unit and its contents, or is that your obligation? Does the facility have sufficient liability and casualty insurance?

CHANGES PERMITTED TO LIVING UNIT

Can you paint any color, replace carpeting and window treatments, install lighting, or change flooring? Are major renovations allowed? Can you move walls, change kitchens and baths? Be sure this is spelled out, otherwise you might be responsible for returning the unit to its original condition when you leave.

RULES AND REGULATIONS

Ask for a copy of the residents' handbook and read it carefully before signing a contract. Make sure there are no rules and regulations that you would find unacceptable. Is smoking permitted in residential units and/or common areas? Is alcohol permitted on the premises? Is there a dress code in the dining room or elsewhere? Are pets allowed, and, if so, what kind? Are overnight guests permitted in apartments? Are visiting hours restricted in any level of care? Are roommates other than spouses or same-sex siblings permitted in apartments?

TRANSFER

Who makes the decision to move you to another level of care? Are you entitled to appeal that decision? If the move is temporary, will you be able to return to your same apartment? Is "temporary" defined?

NONPERFORMANCE

What are the residents' rights if the facility fails to deliver services, provide health care, or maintain the facility as promised?

References

In addition to the credit references mentioned earlier in this chapter, there are other people you should talk to before signing a contract. They include:

- Better Business Bureau (BBB)
- Civic/business leaders
- Current and former residents and families

BETTER BUSINESS BUREAU

The BBB accepts and processes complaints about companies in a local area and investigates claims of fraud. A complaint against a company must be received by the BBB in writing, which, unfortunately, many consumers do not take the time to do. Therefore, just because the BBB has no complaints against a company does not mean that the company has no problems. But you might find that the company has a long history of consumer complaints, so be sure to check.

CIVIC AND BUSINESS LEADERS

Assuming you have gotten a list of the directors or trustees of the facility or its sponsors, ask around in the community about these individuals. Directors and trustees are usually civic and business leaders in a community. What is their reputation among their peers? If you know some of the directors or trustees personally, call and talk to them about the facility, its philosophy, and its financial security.

CURRENT AND FORMER RESIDENTS AND THEIR FAMILIES

Residents of a facility may be your best source of information. If you ask the facility director to provide you with the names of some residents to talk to, the director obviously will put you in touch with those residents who have the nicest things to say. You are better off just talking to people you come in contact with while having a meal at the facility or while waiting in the lobby.

If you or a friend know someone who lives at the facility or the relative of someone who lives there, don't hesitate to call him or her. Most people will be flattered that you are seeking their advice and will speak openly and honestly about the facility.

By all means, contact people you know or know of who have left a facility. Why did they leave? What were the problems? If you know someone whose now-deceased relative lived at the facility, consult him or her. Was the relative happy there? What was the quality of life like? You'll be surprised at some of the important details that people will reveal.

CHECKLIST

Checked Background and Experience of:

_____ developer   _____ manager

_____ owner   _____ sponsor

Obtained Financial Information:

_____ financial statement

      ____ OF FACILITY   ____ OF OWNER

_____ facility operating budget

_____ credit references

_____ checked liens filed against

      ____ FACILITY   ____ MANAGER

      ____ OWNER

_____ checked lawsuits filed against

      ____ FACILITY   ____ MANAGER

      ____ OWNER

Checked License/Certification/Accreditation:

_____ Facility has proper license.

_____ Facility is certified by Medicare.

_____ Facility is certified by Medicaid.

_____ If facility is a continuing-care retirement community,

      _____ is it accredited?

      _____ has it ever applied for accreditation?

      _____ has it applied for accreditation?

      _____ can't it apply because it is too new?

Read the Contract Carefully and Understand the Following:

_____ time limit of contract:

_____ your right to rescind

_____ renewal procedure

_____ fees:

_____ entrance fee

_____ monthly fees

_____ when payments are due

_____ penalties for late payment

_____ consequences of failure to pay

_____ what fees do and do not cover

_____ what's included in residential unit:

_____ what services are included

_____ what health care is included

_____ how much health care is included

_____ how costs may be increased or decreased

_____ refunds:

_____ entrance fee deposit

_____ security deposit

_____ construction deposit

_____ waiting list deposit

_____ termination of contract:

_____ by resident

_____ by facility

_____ insurance coverage

_____ what changes are permitted to residential unit

_____ rules and regulations

_____ have received and read residents' handbook

_____ transfer to other levels of care

_____ nonperformance of facility

Checked Other References:

_____ Better Business Bureau

_____ Talked to directors or trustees.

_____ Talked to other civic and business leaders.

_____ Talked to current residents and/or their families.

_____ Talked to former residents and/or their families.

CHAPTER FIVE

Understanding Medicare, Medicaid, Medigap and Long-Term-Care Insurance

Some portion of the costs of medical care and nursing services at a senior residential facility may be covered by one of the following:

- Medicare
- Medicaid
- Medigap
- Long-term-care insurance

Because each of these topics is extremely complex, this chapter is intended only as a brief introduction to these options and how they may apply to a senior residential facility. The names, addresses, and phone numbers of various private associations and government agencies where you can get more detailed information are listed at the end of the chapter.

If you are looking at senior residential facilities for yourself, you are probably sixty-five years old or more and may already know a lot of this information. But for adult children who are researching options for older family members and who haven't yet had to deal with this part of the health-care maze, we'll start with basic definitions of Medicare, Medicaid, Medigap, and long-term-care insurance, then take a closer look at each topic.

• *Medicare* is federal health insurance for older people, regardless of income, and certain disabled people, regardless of age.
• *Medicaid* is a state-run program that pays for medical care for low-income people of all ages.
• *Medigap* is private health insurance that supplements Medicare coverage by paying certain charges that Medicare doesn't pay.
• *Long-term-care insurance* is private insurance that pays for some long-term-care services, such as home health care and nursing home care.

Medicare

Medicare is a federal health insurance program primarily for people age sixty-five and older, regardless of their income. Certain disabled people and people with permanent kidney failure, regardless of their age, are also eligible to receive Medicare benefits.

The most common misconception about Medicare is that the program will pay all of your medical expenses. That's not true. Medicare is a limited program that pays only a portion of certain expenses.

First, Medicare *shares* the cost of medical care with the *beneficiary* (the person receiving Medicare benefits). In addition, Medicare coverage (what Medicare will pay) is *limited* to some services provided by some people or places under certain circumstances for a limited period of time.

Medicare is divided into two parts. Part A is hospital insurance and is free of charge to most people. Part B, which is medical insurance, is optional coverage that you can buy for a monthly premium.

The Medicare program is administered by the Health Care Financing Administration, which is a part of the U.S. Department of Health and Human Services. Money to pay for Part A hospital insurance benefits comes from payroll taxes paid into the Social Security system by employers and employees. Money to pay for Part B medical insurance benefits comes partly from monthly premiums and partly from general government funds.

Current plans to overhaul the Medicare system will no doubt result in significant changes in the coming years. Beneficiaries' out-of-pocket expenses for premiums, deductibles, and copayments will likely increase. The amount Medicare reimburses doctors, hospitals, and other health-care providers is likely to decrease. Which services are covered and for how long may also change, and beneficiaries will be given incentives to join Health Maintenance Organizations and other private health plans. Overall, however, the concept and terminology will remain intact so that understanding how the system works at this time (1997) will help you understand any changes that later become effective. Let's begin with an overview.

- PART A (hospital insurance) includes:

  - Inpatient hospital care
  - Skilled-nursing care
  - Home health care
  - Hospice care

- PART B (medical insurance) includes:

  - Physician charges
  - Other outpatient services

Enrollment in Medicare may be automatic or you may have to apply for it. Here's how it works. If you or your spouse have retired and are receiving Social Security or railroad retirement benefits, you will be enrolled in Medicare Part A and Part B automatically on your sixty-fifth birthday, and a Medicare card will be mailed to you. If you do *not* want Part B, you will have to notify your local Social Security office.

There is no charge for Part A coverage, but you will have to pay a monthly premium for Part B. The premium can be billed quarterly or deducted from your Social Security or railroad retirement benefits.

If you decide not to get Part B during your initial enrollment period, you will be charged a penalty if you decide to enroll at a later date. You will pay a premium surcharge of 10 percent for each twelve-month period in which you could have enrolled but did not. The surcharge may be waived in certain instances.

Medicare enrollment is not automatic if you are still working when you turn sixty-five, even though you are eligible for Social Security or railroad retirement benefits because you have the necessary work credits of 40 quarters. In that case, you are eligible for Medicare, but you will have to apply for it at your local Social Security office.

If, however, you are sixty-five or older and don't have enough Social Security or railroad retirement work credits, you can still enroll in Medicare, but you'll have to buy into the system by paying monthly premiums. You can buy just Part A, just Part B, or both.

To find out how many work credits you or your spouse has, ask your local Social Security office for a *Request for Earnings and Benefit Estimate Statement.* After completing and mailing the form to the address provided, you will be notified by mail of your status within several weeks.

It is important to understand that Medicare will pay only a portion of your medical expenses. You must pay out-of-pocket:

- Deductibles
- Coinsurance or copayments
- Any excess charges of providers who do not accept Medicare assignment
- Any costs not covered by Medicare

DEDUCTIBLE

A *deductible* is a specified amount that you must pay first before Medicare coverage begins.

- *PART A* has a deductible ($736 in 1996) for each benefit period. A *benefit period* begins on the first day of your hospital stay and ends when you have been out of the hospital or skilled-nursing facility for sixty consecutive days, including the day of discharge. Another benefit period will begin the next time you receive inpatient hospital care.

  The deductible is charged for the first admission to the hospital during the benefit period only. If you are discharged, then readmitted during the benefit period, you do not pay another deductible. There is no limit on the number of benefit periods for hospital and skilled-nursing care.
- *PART B* has an annual deductible ($100 in 1996). You pay that amount only once each year.

COINSURANCE/COPAYMENT

Medicare sets up a payment schedule of specific medical services and what it considers to be a reasonable charge for each service. This reasonable charge, which may vary according to location, is called the *Medicare approved amount* or *allowed amount.*

Medicare pays 80 percent of the approved amount and the beneficiary pays (or copays) the remaining 20 percent, which is called *coinsurance* or *copayment.*

PARTICIPATING AND NONPARTICIPATING PROVIDERS

A *provider* is either a *person* such as a doctor, technician, or therapist who provides medical services; a *place* such as a clinic or hospital that provides medical services; or the *supplier* of medical equipment.

Participating providers are those who choose to participate in the Medicare system, thereby agreeing to accept the Medicare-approved amount for services to Medicare patients. Once deductibles have been met, the beneficiary pays the 20 percent coinsurance charge at the time of service, and the provider files a claim with Medicare for Medicare's 80 percent share of the approved amount. Medicare then assigns its payment directly to the provider. This is called *accepting Medicare assignment*, or simply accepting assignment.

Providers who do not agree to accept the Medicare-approved amount as payment in full for services rendered are called *nonparticipating* providers. If your provider is nonparticipating, you must pay the full bill at the time of service. Medicare will reimburse you 80 percent of the approved amount after the doctor files your claim, but there's a catch. The approved amount for nonparticipating providers is 5 percent less than the approved amount for participating providers, which is Medicare's way of encouraging providers to participate. So in addition to the 20 percent coinsurance charge, you pay the difference between the lower Medicare-approved amount and the actual charge. However, federal law limits what nonparticipating physicians can charge to 15 percent above the Medicare-approved amount, and any overcharges must be refunded.

For example, a participating doctor may normally charge $400 for a particular medical procedure, but the Medicare-approved amount for that procedure is $300. Medicare reimburses the doctor 80 percent or $240, and the patient pays the remaining 20 percent (coinsurance) or $60.

If the doctor is nonparticipating, however, the Medicare approved amount for that same $400 procedure is only $285 (5 percent less than the $300 approved amount for participating doctors). Medicare limits what the doctor can charge to $327.75 (15 percent above the approved amount of $285). Since Medicare does not reimburse the nonparticipating doctor directly, the patient is responsible for paying the full bill of $327.75. The doctor will file the claim for the patient, then Medicare will reimburse the patient $228, which is 80 percent of the $285 approved amount (not 80 percent of the total bill).

In this example, the patient of the participating doctor ends up paying $60 out of pocket, while the patient of the nonparticipating doctor ends up paying $99.75 out of pocket.

Patients should know that some nonparticipating providers, if asked, will agree to accept the Medicare-approved amount on an individual basis.

You can get a free copy of the *Medicare Participating Physicians and Suppliers Directory* (also called *MEDPARD Directory*) from your state Medicare carrier. *Medicare carriers,* which are commercial insurance companies that contract with the Health Care Financing Administration to process Medicare Part B claims, are listed in *Your Medicare Handbook.*

Now that you understand the basics of Medicare, let's look more closely at what Part A and Part B include. Remember, Part A, which most people sixty-five and older get premium-free, covers inpatient hospital care, skilled-nursing care, home health care, and hospice care. Part B, which is optional and requires payment of a monthly premium, covers physician charges and other outpatient services.

MEDICARE PART A

INPATIENT HOSPITAL CARE (Covers 150 Days per Stay)
You pay a deductible of $736 (1996) for each benefit period. After the deductible, Medicare will pay:

• *For days 1–60:* 100 percent of all eligible charges.
• *For days 61–90:* All eligible charges, except $184 a day.
• *For days 91–150:* All eligible charges except $368 a day for a total of 60 days that can be used only once in a lifetime. The 60 once-in-a-lifetime days are called *reserve days.*

Let's say, for example, that you stay in the hospital 100 days. You pay a deductible of $736, then Medicare will pay 100 percent of all eligible charges for the first sixty days. For days sixty-one through ninety, you pay $184 per day and Medicare will pick up the remaining eligible charges. You may choose to use ten of your once-in-a-lifetime reserve days for days ninety through one hundred, in which case you pay $368 a day for those days, and Medicare will cover the remaining eligible charges. You will still have fifty reserve days left for future use.

Hospital charges Medicare will pay:

- A semiprivate room
- All meals, including special diets
- Regular nursing services
- Costs of special-care units, such as intensive-care or coronary-care units
- Drugs furnished during your stay
- Lab tests included in your hospital bill
- X rays and radiation therapy included in your hospital bill
- Medical supplies such as casts, surgical dressings, and splints
- Use of appliances such as a wheelchair
- Operating- and recovery-room costs
- Physical, speech, and occupational therapy
- Blood transfusions furnished by the hospital, except for the first three pints of blood per calendar year

Hospital charges Medicare will not pay:

- Television
- Telephone
- Private-duty nurses
- Private room unless deemed medically necessary

Note that Part A does not pay for the physician services you receive while in the hospital. Those charges are covered by Part B, if you have it.

SKILLED-NURSING FACILITY (Covers 100 Days per Benefit Period)

Medicare will pay for skilled-nursing care only if *all* five of the following conditions are met:

- You must be hospitalized for at least three consecutive days (not counting the day of discharge) before entering a Medicare-certified skilled-nursing facility.
- You must be admitted to the skilled-nursing facility within a short time (generally thirty days) after you leave the hospital.
- Your care in the skilled-nursing facility is for a condition that was treated in the hospital.
- Your condition requires daily skilled-nursing or skilled-rehabilitation services *(not custodial care)* that can be provided only in a skilled-nursing facility.
- A medical professional certifies that you need and receive these skilled-nursing services on a daily basis.

If those conditions are met, Medicare will pay:

- *For days 1–20:* 100 percent of eligible charges
- *For days 21–100:* All eligible charges except $92 per day. Medicare pays nothing after 100 days.

If you leave a skilled-nursing facility before your 100 days are used up and are readmitted within the same benefit period for treatment of the same condition, Medicare will continue coverage. In that instance, a new three-day prior hospital stay is not required.

What Medicare will pay for in a skilled-nursing facility:

- Semiprivate room.
- All meals, including special diet
- Regular nursing services
- Physical, occupational, speech therapy
- Drugs furnished during your stay
- Blood transfusions during your stay, except the first three pints of blood per calendar year
- Medical supplies such as casts and splints
- Use of appliances such as a wheelchair

What Medicare will not pay for in a skilled-nursing facility:

- Television
- Telephone
- Private-duty nurses
- Private room unless deemed medically necessary

HOME HEALTH CARE (no limit on days)

Medicare will pay for part-time or intermittent home health care for treatment of an illness or injury if *all* four of the following conditions are met:

- You are confined to your home.
- Your physician determines that you need home health care and sets up a home health plan for you.
- The care you need includes intermittent skilled-nursing care, physical therapy, or speech therapy.
- The home health agency providing services participates in Medicare.

If those conditions are met, Medicare will pay 100 percent of the approved amount for as long as needed and 80 percent of the approved amount for *durable medical equipment* such as wheelchairs, oxygen equipment, and other reusable medical equipment appropriate for home use.

Home health services that Medicare will not pay for include twenty-four-hour nursing care, drugs and biologicals, home-delivered meals, homemaker services (cleaning and cooking), and blood transfusions.

HOSPICE CARE (Covers 210 Days)

Hospice is a program of noncurative care that provides pain relief, symptom management, and support to terminally ill patients and their families. The goal of hospice is to let people die at home with as little pain as possible, but, when necessary, care can be provided in an inpatient hospice unit, hospital, or nursing facility.

Medicare will pay for up to 210 days of hospice care for terminally ill patients in a Medicare-participating hospice program. There are no deductibles for hospice care.

MEDICARE PART B

After the annual deductible of $100 (1996), Medicare will pay 80 percent of the approved costs of:

- Physician services
- Outpatient hospital care
- Outpatient speech therapy
- Outpatient physical therapy
- Laboratory tests
- Outpatient mental health services
- Ambulance service
- Annual flu shots
- Mammography screening every other year
- Podiatrist treatment of infected toenails
- Chiropractor's spinal manipulation (if treatment is indicated by X ray)
- Treatment of cataracts by an optometrist
- Prosthetic devices
- Therapeutic shoes for severe diabetic foot disease

In general, there is no limit to the number of days of care covered as long as the service or treatment is deemed medically necessary.

Part B does not pay for:

• Most outpatient prescription drugs
• Dental plates or other dental devices

MANAGED-CARE HEALTH PLANS

A *managed-care health plan* is a prepaid health plan that provides medical services, as well as preventative care, to members for a fixed premium. Some plans call for small deductibles and/or copayments, but basically the premium covers whatever amount of care the member receives. Members (usually called *subscribers*) are limited to using only those doctors and facilities that are affiliated with the particular managed-care plan. Plans are set up in different ways. Some have their own facilities and salaried doctors, while others contract with group practices or doctors in private practice to provide health care to their subscribers.

Medicare beneficiaries enrolled in Part B who live in an area served by a managed-care plan that has a contract with Medicare may choose to enroll in such a plan. This is an alternative to receiving Medicare benefits through the regular fee-for-service system. You must still pay the Medicare Part B premium, but the advantage of a managed-care plan is that you don't have to pay Medicare's deductibles or worry about benefit periods. In addition, most managed-care plans provide extra benefits not provided by Medicare, such as routine physicals, eye exams, and prescription drugs for little or no extra fee. The disadvantage is that you are limited to using only those doctors and hospitals in the plan's network.

For more information on Medicare, consult the current issue of *Your Medicare Handbook*, the government publication that outlines in detail the specifics of the federal program. Call your local Social Security office or the national Social Security toll-free number (800-772-1213) to request a free copy of the handbook.

Medicaid

Medicaid is a medical assistance program that pays the cost of medical care for people of all ages with low income and low assets. It is important to understand Medicaid because (unlike Medicare) it pays for long-term nursing care. In fact, Medicaid pays nearly half of all nursing home costs in the United States.

Medicaid was established by Congress in 1965 as part of the Social Security Act. Money to fund Medicaid comes from the federal, state, and local governments, but each state designs and runs its own Medicaid program. As a result, eligibility requirements and services vary from state to state. So does the agency that administers the program. Call your local welfare or Social Security office to find out which agency administers Medicaid in your state. That agency can explain your state's eligibility requirements, including income and asset limits. There is no residency requirement. You can apply for Medicaid in any state in which you currently reside.

Don't discount the possibility of being eligible for Medicaid just because your income is above the Medicaid limit. Some states extend benefits to people defined as *medically needy*. You might be eligible for Medicaid even if your income exceeds the Medicaid limit when your medical costs are very high in relation to your income. You are deemed medically needy if your net income falls below the Medicaid limit once you subtract your medical expenses.

To be eligible for Medicaid you must meet both income *and* asset requirements.

- *Income* is any money received in a given period such as wages, pensions, cash benefits, rent, etc.
- *Assets* are things you own that have value such as property, cars, insurance policies, jewelry, cash, savings account, stocks, and bonds.

Some limited assets such as a house and car of reasonable value, household goods, burial space, and funeral funds are not counted when determining your Medicaid eligibility.

If your income is low enough for you to qualify for Medicaid, but the value of your assets is too high, you can still become eligible for Medicaid for long-term-nursing care by means of a "spend down." *Spend down* means that you use your assets to pay for medical and nursing care until those assets are reduced or "spent down" below the state's Medicaid limit.

Some people transfer or give away some of their assets in order to be eligible for Medicaid, but that must be done at least 30 months before applying for Medicaid. Talk to your lawyer about the best ways to do this.

Recent changes in the law now allow a spouse to keep some income and assets when the other spouse is receiving Medicaid assistance for long-term care in a nursing facility. This protects the spouse living at home from being impoverished. The amount that the spouse can keep is adjusted upward each year for inflation.

Note that it is easier to enter a nursing facility as a private-pay patient, but if it's a Medicaid-certified facility you cannot be discharged once you become eligible for Medicaid. If no Medicaid bed is available, however, the facility may be allowed to transfer you to another facility.

Basic medical services covered by Medicaid:

- Inpatient hospital services
- Skilled-nursing services
- Outpatient lab, X-ray services
- Physician services for office visits, care in hospital, treatment in hospital outpatient clinics
- Outpatient hospital services
- Home health services, equipment, and supplies
- Family planning services
- Special child health services (health checkups, immunizations, diagnosis, and treatment)

Additional things covered by Medicaid in some states:

- Prescription drugs
- Dental services
- Eyeglasses
- Private-duty nursing
- Clinics
- Prosthetic devices
- Physical therapy
- Emergency room
- Optometrists
- Podiatrists
- Chiropractors
- Mental hospitals
- Ambulance services

Medigap

The term *Medigap* refers to a number of Medicare-supplement insurance policies sold by private insurance companies. A Medigap policy supplements Medicare coverage. Another way of saying it is that a Medigap policy helps fill in the gaps of Medicare coverage. Those gaps are what Medicare beneficiaries pay out of pocket. Recall from a previous discussion that Medicare will pay only a portion of your medical expenses. You must pay:

- Deductibles
- Coinsurance or copayments
- An additional amount to providers who do not accept Medicare assignment
- Any costs not covered by Medicare (such as private room, private-duty nurse, prescription drugs, routine medical exams, etc.)

Those are the gaps filled in by Medigap policies in varying degrees, depending on the policy you buy. You must have both Part A and Part B Medicare to buy a Medigap policy.

Medigap policies in most states now conform to ten standard benefit plans developed by the National Association of Insurance Commissioners, a nonprofit association whose members are the chief regulatory officials in all states, the District of Columbia, and the U.S. territories.

The benefit plans, designed to make comparison shopping by consumers easier, are designated by the letters *A* through *J*. Plan A provides the least coverage and is the least expensive, while Plan J provides maximum coverage and is usually the most expensive.

The ten plans include one or more of the following benefit packages:

1. Basic benefits (included in all ten plans) pays:
   - Coinsurance costs for Part A inpatient hospital stays
   - 100 percent of the cost of hospital stay for up to 365 additional days per lifetime
   - Coinsurance costs for Part B medical expenses
   - The cost of the first three pints of blood used each year
2. Part A inpatient hospital deductible
3. Part A skilled nursing coinsurance
4. Part B deductible
5. Foreign travel emergency
6. At-home recovery
7. Part B excess physician charges
8. Preventive screening
9. Outpatient prescription drugs

There are other standard Medigap practices mandated by law. All insurance companies are required to use the same wording to describe benefits and are required to offer certain benefits in each plan (though insurers can add benefits). A maximum price that companies can charge for specific benefits is also set by law.

This standardization makes it easier for consumers to compare policies, but there still are some snags. Insurance companies use different methods of calculating premiums and include a variety of extra benefits that are not regulated by the government. Consequently, prices vary dramatically (up to 100 percent in some cases) for the same coverage. So shop around!

Once you buy a policy you have a 30-day free-look period, which means you can cancel the policy within 30 days from the time you buy it and receive a full refund.

Long-Term-Care Insurance

Long-term-care insurance is a relatively new offspring of the insurance industry. Sold by private insurance companies, long-term-care policies cover the cost of caring for people who cannot take care of themselves because they are too ill, frail, or otherwise disabled.

Health insurance pays medical expenses, while long-term-care insurance pays for caregiving. That care may be provided in a nursing home or in an individual's home by a home-care agency. Some policies also cover care in community facilities such as adult day-care centers.

Long-term-care insurance can be expensive, with premiums costing several hundred to several thousand dollars a year. Your age and health are factors to consider when buying long-term-care insurance, but your ability to pay the premiums now *and* in the future should be your primary concern.

Even though you might be able to afford a $1,500 annual premium now, you may be forced to drop the policy later when you really need it because the increased premium is no longer affordable on your fixed income. Depending on your policy, you may or may not get back some of your investment.

Unlike Medigap, long-term-care insurance has not been standardized, making it more difficult for consumers to comparison shop. Nevertheless, it is essential that you do so. Whether you buy from an insurance agent, from your employer, or directly from an insurance company that advertises through the mail or on television, you should compare several policies to determine what coverage is best for you and what will fit into your financial planning for the future.

Many employers have begun offering their employees the opportunity to buy long-term-care insurance for themselves and for their parents. These group policies often provide better coverage at a lower price.

The cost of a long-term-care policy will be determined by a number of factors:

- Your age at the time you buy the policy
- Benefits included
- Benefit period (how long benefits last)
- Benefit waiting period (how long before benefits begin)
- Conditions under which benefits will be paid
- Renewability of the policy
- Other optional benefits included

AGE

The older you are when you buy long-term-care insurance, the more expensive your premium is likely to be. If you buy a policy at age seventy-five, you will pay about 2½ times more than if you had bought the same policy at age sixty-five, and six times more than if you had bought it at age fifty-five.*

---

* National Association of Insurance Commissioners, *A Shopper's Guide to Long-Term-Care Insurance* (Kansas City: National Association of Insurance Commissioners, 1993), p. 22.

BENEFITS

1. What services are covered?
   - Home care
   - Nursing care (custodial, intermediate or skilled care?)
   - Adult day-care centers
   - Other community facilities
2. Where are those services covered?
   - In any state licensed facility
   - In specific kinds of facilities only
3. How much are daily benefits and how are they calculated?
   - Fixed dollar amount for each day of care received
   - A percentage of the cost of services
   - A specified dollar amount to cover actual charges for services
   - Does the policy have an *inflation protection clause* that provides for benefit increases over time? Such protection will increase the cost of your premium considerably.

BENEFIT PERIOD

How long do the benefits last? Will your policy pay for a one-year, five-year, or lifetime nursing home stay? You will pay more for longer benefit periods.

BENEFIT WAITING PERIOD

The length of time you have to wait before the insurance company will begin paying for your care is called an *elimination period*. For example, your policy may state that care in a skilled-nursing facility won't begin until the seventh day of your stay. The shorter the elimination period, the more expensive the premium will be. Some policies have no elimination period, which is even more costly.

CONDITIONS UNDER WHICH BENEFITS WILL BE PAID

Your policy may offer certain benefits, but then restrict the conditions under which those benefits will be paid. These restrictions, called *gatekeepers,* include such things as:

- Your care must be ordered by a doctor.
- Your care is required as a result of sickness or injury (which would exclude custodial care).
- You must have been in the hospital for a minimum of three days before you can qualify for benefits.
- You cannot perform certain activities of daily living (bathing, eating, dressing, walking, going to the toilet, transferring from bed to chair) without help from someone.
- You cannot perform certain activities of daily living without supervision.

RENEWABILITY

Be sure you understand whether or not the policy can be renewed at the end of the term for which it was written. Your policy may be:

- *Renewable* for life at your discretion.
- *Guaranteed renewable* at your discretion until you reach a specified age. (The insurance company can increase the premium.)
- *Optionally renewable* at the discretion of the insurance company.
- *Nonrenewable* (also called *term*)—the policy cannot be renewed.

OTHER OPTIONAL BENEFITS

There are several optional benefits that can add to the cost of your policy, for example:

- *Death benefits:* Your estate will be refunded the premiums you paid, less any benefits the insurance company paid out on your policy.
- *Nonforfeiture benefits:* If you drop your policy after a certain number of years and never used any of the policy's coverage, you will get some of your investment back.

The National Association of Insurance Commissioners publishes a booklet called *A Shopper's Guide to Long-Term-Care Insurance* that explains in detail the various aspects of long-term-care insurance. State law requires insurance companies to give you the guide when you buy long-term-care insurance.

Anybody buying a Medigap or long-term-care policy (or any type of health insurance) should check with the state department of insurance to be sure the insurance company is licensed by the state. You should also check the company's rating by a private insurance rating company, such as A. M. Best and Co., which rates insurance companies based on their financial strength. A. M. Best and Co. publishes a book called *Best's Insurance Reports* that should be available in your local library.

RESOURCES
AARP Fulfillment
601 E Street, N.W.
Washington, DC 20049

Write for single free copy of the following publications; include title and publication number: *Before You Buy: A Guide to Long-Term-Care Insurance* (#D12893)—a consumer guide to evaluating long-term-care policies. Gives general advice and guidelines. *Medicare: What It Covers, What It Doesn't* (#D13133)—describes Medicare coverage.

A.M. Best and Co.
Ambest Road
Oldwick, NJ 08858
908–439–2200
908–439–3296 (fax)
800–424–2378

Call for rating of insurance company or check *Best's Insurance Reports* at your library.

Health Insurance Association of America
555 13th Street, N.W.
Suite 600 East
Washington, DC 20004–1109

Write for free publications on health insurance and free listing by state of insurance companies that sell long-term-care insurance.

Medicare Hotline
800–638–6833

Call with questions about Medicare coverage, 8:00 A.M. to 8:00 P.M. (EST), Monday through Friday.

National Association Insurance Commissioners
120 West 12th Street,
Suite 1100
Kansas City, MO 64105–1925

Write for free copy of *A Shopper's Guide to Long-Term-Care Insurance* and *Guide to Health Insurance for People with Medicare.*

National Insurance Consumers Helpline
800–942–4242

Will answer specific questions, provide referrals, and mail

free educational materials on life, health, auto, home, and business insurance.

People's Medical Society
462 Walnut Street
Allentown, PA 18102
610–770–1670
A nonprofit consumer organization that answers questions, provides referrals, and publishes a variety of publications aimed at educating consumers about their medical rights.

Social Security Administration
800–772–1213

Call to see if you or your spouse have worked long enough under Social Security, railroad retirement, as a government employee, or a combination of those systems to be eligible for Medicare Part A benefits. Order free current copy of *Your Medicare Handbook.*

State Departments of Insurance
(See Appendix D for listing by state of departments of insurance and insurance counseling offices.)

- Answer questions on Medicare, Medicaid, Medigap, and long-term-care insurance.
- Provide help in choosing health insurance coverage.
- Provide help in understanding insurance bills and claims.
- Provide free printed information on different types of health insurance.

United Seniors Health Cooperative
1331 H Street, N.W.
Suite 500
Washington, DC. 20005
202–393–6222

Provides publications on Medicare, Medigap, and long-term-care insurance.

CHAPTER SIX

Making the Move

So now what? The process that began with making the decision to move yourself or a family member to a senior residential facility is nearly complete. You've researched the options, chosen the one that best fits your circumstances, and completed a thorough check of the facility. All that seems left to do now is move. Some might think that's the easy part; just call the movers and start packing. But it's not so simple.

The physical details of moving require a lot of organization and preparation, particularly for someone who has seventy or eighty years of acquisitions that span the spectrum from junk to necessities to valuables to cherished memorabilia.

But don't forget the psychological preparation necessary for a move to be successful. Even in the best of circumstances, moving is considered one of life's most stressful situations. Some child-rearing books dedicate pages or even chapters to helping young children cope with the psychological trauma of moving. Why should a move be any less traumatic for an elderly person who is leaving a familiar, comfortable environment to enter a strange new one at a time when he or she most needs security?

This chapter will discuss the physical and psychological aspects of moving and give tips on how to make the move easier.

Psychological

If you are helping an elderly family member move, chances are you are a baby boomer who has moved numerous times in your life. Like many of your highly mobile generation, you may have gone to college and moved around from a dormitory to an apartment, changed schools, moved home for a while, had jobs in different cities, moved up in the rental market, bought a home and then traded up for a larger one in a better neighborhood. A divorce may have forced you back into the rental market or into a smaller house, and a remarriage may have resulted in another move. By this time in your life moving may be no big deal—a physical hassle, surely, but not a psychological trauma.

Now consider your parents or grandparents. If they went to college at all they may have lived at home while doing so. If they went away to school they probably lived in a dormitory, not an apartment, before returning to their hometown to settle down. And settle down is just what their generation did, typically working at the same company and living in the same neighborhood (and maybe the same house) for decades. Having lived through a world war and the Great Depression, they sought emotional and financial security. Moving around in search of excitement, better jobs, new relationships, and adventure was the furthest thing from their minds. Their goal was to put down roots, while moving, by definition, is uprooting.

Imagine how difficult it is for someone who has lived in the same neighborhood for fifty years or the same house for thirty years to move to a new home. To make matters worse, that new home may be in a different city or state, possibly in a different climate, or even in a different type of building. For someone who has lived in a one- or two-story house all of his or her life, making the adjustment to high-rise living may be difficult.

What if, on top of all that, your parent or grandparent has just lost a spouse after fifty years of marriage and will be making this move alone? Not only will he or she be uprooted from familiar surroundings, but he or she will be uprooted from the past and all the things that evoke a lifetime of cherished memories. A deep sense of loss is inevitable.

Whether it is you or a family member who is making the move, the first step to making the psychological adjustment easier is to recognize and accept the difficulties involved. Most elderly people are fully aware of the numerous losses that come with aging, but their adult children who are still acquiring, accomplishing, and advancing in life may not have given the subject much thought. Consider for a minute just some of these significant losses:

- Agility
- Youthfulness
- Vision or hearing
- Memory
- Hair or teeth
- Family unit (children move away)
- Spouse (death or divorce)
- Friends (who die)
- Companionship (loss of spouse/friends)
- Social interaction
- Independence
- Job/career
- Self-esteem (derived from career or raising a family)
- Financial security

In addition to these losses, which most elderly people have to cope with and adjust to, the move to a senior residential facility causes other losses, such as the loss of:

- Home (and the memories it held)
- Familiar surroundings

- Support network (of nearby friends and neighbors)
- Privacy

All of these losses cause stress and require good coping skills, a positive attitude, and the willingness to adapt to change. Those who have not developed these through a lifetime of experience will have the most difficulty moving at this stage in their lives.

Others, however, may view the move as liberating—an opportunity to free themselves from the burden of owning and having to look after so many things, as well as the burden of maintaining a house and yard. They may look forward to meeting new friends and getting involved in new activities. They may feel relieved to be living in a secure environment where they no longer have to worry about their physical safety and access to health care. For these people, moving to a residential facility may mean increased independence and less reliance on children and friends for help.

Whatever the personality type of the person making the move, it is important to discuss openly the inevitable sense of loss, anxieties, and fears involved in the move. That may be difficult for Mom or Dad, whose generation tends to be more emotionally guarded or reserved than that of their adult children. But it may also be difficult for adult children who either feel guilty about the move or just feel uncomfortable seeing their parent in such a vulnerable position.

Don't make the mistake of thinking that because the move is necessary or inevitable that there's no point in stirring up negative feelings. "Let's just get it over and done with and act as if everyone is happy." Nothing could be further from the truth. Remember that just talking about something relieves a lot of stress and often makes that which is feared less fearful.

Having your feelings recognized and validated by someone else helps you cope with those feelings and makes it easier to move on. A simple statement, such as "Mom, it must be very sad for you to leave the house that you and Dad shared for so many years," or "Gee, Dad, it must be scary to move and have to make new friends for the first time without Mom," will go a long way in helping your parents deal with their own feelings. Just as children need acceptance and recognition by their parents, so do parents need acceptance and recognition by their children. It will be a lot easier for your parents to make the adjustment if they know you are giving them emotional support through this difficult time.

Besides, you may be surprised at the response! Mom may say, "Yes, it's sad, but I have wanted to get out of that old house for years. It was Dad who never wanted to move." Dad may respond, "Actually, I'm kind of looking forward to making my own friends. Mom was always the one who chose our friends."

In addition to talking with elderly family members about their feelings, it is important to get them involved in the decision-making process as early as possible. Even if you are dealing with reluctant or contrary family members, it is best to discuss the move, explain the options, take them on visits when possible (letting them see and speak for themselves), and seek their input. They may slowly come to accept the inevitable and at least feel they have not been stripped of all control.

Once the decision has been made, the person moving should be involved in choosing which living unit he or she prefers (if there is a choice), how it will be decorated, and what furniture to bring. Many dutiful children think they are doing their parents a great service by completely decorating the new residence for them, but that may actually make the transition more difficult. The new place may be beautiful, but it won't feel like home.

You may have always hated the green color of Mom and Dad's living room and can't wait to paint the new apartment blue and update some of their furnishings. But to Mom and Dad, that color green and the worn armchair may be important elements of "home" and emotional security. If your parents are not up to the physical task of decorating their own apartment, ask them what they want. Let them select paint colors. Bring them fabric samples to choose from. Ask what furniture they want to bring and what they want to dispose of. Let them decide where the furniture should be placed. Remember, they will be living there, not you. And don't forget to solicit Dad's opinion if he is moving alone. Even Dads have decorating likes and dislikes. It may be the first time ever that he is able to choose his favorite color!

Child psychologists advise parents of toddlers to get the youngsters involved in a move as much as possible. Talk about the upcoming event, let the children help select things for their new room, and let them see the activity on moving day. All that helps make the psychological transition to the new home easier. It is really no different with elderly parents.

Another help in easing the transition is to visit the facility several times before the move. Walk around, become as familiar with the new physical surroundings as possible. Even the slightest feeling of familiarity will help. Visit with staff and residents of the facility, introduce yourself or your family member as a soon-to-be new resident.

Perhaps your mother is moving to a facility in your hometown where she knows no one. Have her stay with you for a while and visit the facility several times before she moves in. If some of your friends have relatives or friends who live at the facility, plan a coffee, tea, or cocktail party at your home or at the facility to introduce Mom to a few people ahead of time.

If you are moving to a new town or even a new neighborhood in your hometown, take time to become familiar with the surrounding area before the move. Get a map of the area. Even if you won't be driving, it is psychologically important to know the area, street names, proximity to other neighborhoods, and general lay of the land.

Start by exploring the area immediately surrounding the facility, then widen the circle. Locate the nearest hospital, church, bank, grocery, pharmacy, shops, dry cleaner, etc. Go to the grocery and apply for a check-cashing card. Stop in at the pharmacy and meet the pharmacist. Open a checking account at the bank. Attend a church service and introduce yourself to the clergy. Again, the more familiarity you can develop before the move, the easier the move will be. It is difficult at any age to simply wake up one day in new surroundings and not have a sense of where you are and what's around you.

So remember, this is a major change in your life or the life of your family member. Take the time for the important psychological preparations.

- Talk about fears, losses, changes
- Involve the person who is moving as much as possible
- Develop familiarity with the facility and surrounding area before the move
- Meet staff and residents before the move

Physical

Let's face it, moving is just one of life's dreaded chores. There is nothing pleasant about sorting through, packing, moving, unpacking, and rearranging all of one's things. It takes its toll on even the most organized and most energetic person, but an older person who has less physical and mental stamina can be overwhelmed by the process.

Maybe you have already made a major move from the larger family home to a smaller house or apartment and have rid yourself of numerous possessions along the way. Consider yourself fortunate! Many people at this stage, however, are faced with scaling down from a three-bedroom house with a lot of basement, closet, and attic storage to a one-bedroom apartment. How do you begin to sort through a lifetime of accumulation, not to mention the myriad other details and arrangements associated with a move?

Anyone who has ever moved knows that moving is a process, not just an event that takes place on moving day. The problem is that most people forget how much time that process takes. Just as it is important to take the time to prepare psychologically for the move, it is important to spend time on physical preparations.

THROWING OUT AND ORGANIZING

Ideally, those preparations will begin at a leisurely pace months and months in advance as you sort through and organize your things. Bring one or two good boxes home from every trip to the grocery, and begin preparing mentally for the cleaning-out process. People who have spent a lifetime collecting and hoarding things from old magazines and rubber bands to china figurines need to change their mind-set. This is a time of letting go and moving on. Most people find it actually quite liberating.

Start by throwing out clutter and junk. Plan in advance to set aside a few hours on a certain day and schedule your other activities around that time. Start in the least-used room in the house, such as a guest bedroom. Turn on the television or radio and spend an hour or two going through drawers and closets. Divide things into piles: throw away, give away, and sale. At the end of your allotted time, put the things in the throwaway pile in garbage bags and place the bags out for pickup. Arrange the giveaway and sale piles neatly in a corner, then walk out of the room and close the door.

This process is best done away from the watchful eye of a spouse or other family member who may be inclined to root through the garbage bags and your neat piles. Once you've made the decision to get rid of something the last thing you need is someone else picking over each item exclaiming, "You're not going to throw *this* away!" *This* is usually something that hasn't been used or even seen in years.

Don't disregard, however, the sentimental attachment your spouse might have for some things. You may be the one responsible for cleaning out and organizing, but your spouse is just as likely to be undergoing the same psychological trauma about the move as you. Throw out the junk, but set aside any questionable items, and then solicit your spouse's opinion.

Over the next few weeks as you work your way through the various rooms in your home, end each work period by discarding the throwaway pile and moving the items in the giveaway and sale piles to one room. By piling everything in one room, you avoid the clutter and disarray of having things strewn about your house. By the time you've gone through every room in the house, you will have cleaned out a lot, taken a mental inventory of what you have, and you will end up with one or two large piles of things to sell or give away. Note that at this point you are only going through clothes, books, and small items, not furniture. That will come later.

The next step is sorting through the giveaway pile. If you have a sale pile, leave it for now. Divide the giveaway pile into several piles: the children, other special people, and charities or other organizations. If it is easy to designate which child gets which item, make a pile for each child. If, however, you have to stop and think about each item, just make one large "children" pile that you will subdivide later.

You might be one of those people who have a lot of different charities and organizations that you'd like to make donations to, but keep it simple. Choose an organization that will pick up items at your house and at your convenience, and call for pickup as soon as the giveaway pile is big enough. Most organizations that accept donations will be delighted to get your things and will make as many trips as necessary. If you're giving to a charity, be sure to get a tax-deduction receipt.

Distribute any items in your giveaway pile that you have designated for friends, siblings, etc. Ask those people to pick up their gifts, but, if necessary, deliver them yourself. The goal is to get as much out of your house as possible. Getting rid of things is like losing weight—the more results you see, the more encouraged you will be to continue.

If the "children" pile has already been divided up, call any children living in your town and set up a time for them to pick up their things. If possible, have in-town children mail things to their out-of-town siblings. If that's not possible and you can't mail the items yourself, pack them in boxes marked with each child's name and store them out of the way.

If you weren't able to subdivide the "children" pile earlier, now is the time to do so. Get boxes and mark with each child's name. Many people have great difficulty parting with sentimental memorabilia such as childhood scrapbooks, photos, letters, drawings, etc. This can be emotional. Set aside only an hour or two at a time to go through things that you know will stir up memories and emotions, but don't neglect those emotions. As you sort through those special things, savor each memory and shed a few tears if you want. Then put the items in the box and pass them on to your children. They will probably be thrilled to get these bits of their own history, and what they don't want they can discard.

HAVING A SALE

If you are gathering items to sell at a garage or estate sale, let that pile continue to grow until you get closer to moving time, but you need to think through the sale process now and consider several factors.

- Do you plan to have a garage sale yourself or hire someone to sell the items for you? Individuals or companies that perform this service take a percentage of the sale proceeds. That percentage varies, and you should shop around for the best deal.
- If you hire someone, what type of things will they sell? Some estate sale companies accept only furnishings and nicer items, others will sell anything, including typical garage sale junk.
- Where will the sale be held—at your house or at another location?
- When will the sale be held? You might want to wait until right before you move if you're holding the garage sale yourself, or right after you move if you're hiring someone so that any last-minute discards can be included. If you wait until after all the giveaway items are divided up among the children and family members, anything they don't want can be included in the sale.
- How much does clutter bother you? Do you have sufficient out-of-the-way space to accumulate sale items? You might prefer to have the sale sooner than later just to clear things out. Any last-minute things can be thrown away or donated.
- Why are you selling items? If you're really doing it for the money, by waiting you run the risk of having your children pick through and asking for your best sale items.
- Maybe money is not the issue, but your personality type or upbringing simply won't allow you to throw out anything. Think about whether or not you really need or can handle this stress in your life right now. A garage sale at home is a lot of work. Even if you're hiring someone to have the sale for you, you still need to organize and accumulate the things. You might be better off sending everything to the church rummage sale. If, however, you're determined to have a sale yourself, consider letting your grandchildren or neigh-

borhood youngsters take it on as a project for a percentage of the proceeds.

- If you have some more valuable items too good to sell at a garage sale, take them to an antique or consignment shop. Don't wait until you have a carload; take the items to the shop as you collect them. Unless the shop is a considerable distance from your house, it is usually easier to make several trips with one or two items at a time. The longer something sits around your house, the more likely it is to get broken or to cause you to have second thoughts about it.

PLANNING AHEAD

Now is also the time to get serious about organizing the things that you plan to keep, such as photographs, files and important papers. Get a portable file box, preferably fireproof, and organize your records:

- Birth certificate
- Marriage certificate
- Death certificate of spouse
- Divorce papers
- Passport/Citizenship papers
- Military discharge records
- Will
- Living will
- Bank accounts (checking and savings)
- Safe-deposit box
- Social Security
- Stocks/bonds/Mutual funds/Certificates of deposit
- Pension funds/retirement account
- Life insurance
- Health insurance
- Medicare/Medicaid
- Property insurance
- Burial insurance/plot deed
- Income tax (federal and state returns)
- Automobile title/maintenance

- Real estate deeds/titles, etc.
- Inventory of valuables

It will take a while to get everything unpacked and organized once you move, but these important papers should be easily accessible. Also box and mark letters and photographs that you want to keep.

There are a number of other details that you should begin taking care of at least six to eight weeks before you move.

1. *Notify the following of address change:*
    - Post office
    - Social Security
    - Medicare
    - Insurance companies
    - Medical records
    - Driver's license
    - Voter registration
    - Passport
    - Credit cards
    - Charge accounts (Close accounts you won't be using.)
    - Magazines/newspapers (Cancel subscriptions you no longer want.)

2. *Telephone/utilities/cable:* Notify of moving date and request deposit refunds.

3. *Bank:* Notify bank of address change. Order new checks printed with new address. If moving out of town, close bank account. Don't forget your safe-deposit box.

4. *Home services:* Cancel pest control, water delivery, yard service.

5. *Moving companies:* Call several for estimates. Check moving company references and insurance. Call the Better Business Bureau and ask if any complaints have been filed against the company.

6. *Moving announcements:* Order announcements of

move and address change to mail to family and friends.

7. *Stationery:* Order new stationery.

8. *Set up new services:* If necessary, arrange for utility, water, telephone and cable service at new residence, though most facilities take care of those arrangements.

9. *Schedule out-of-town visit:* If moving out of town, schedule a visit ahead of time to do the following:

- Open bank account
- Get safe-deposit box
- Apply for check cashing card at nearby grocery
- Open charge accounts
- Get new driver's license
- Change voter registration

CHOOSING FURNITURE

As it gets closer to moving time, you should know the size and layout of your future residence. Now you need to start thinking about what furniture you will take with you. If you are moving to a facility that offers moving consultation or interior design service, take advantage of it. A consultant will come to your home and advise you about what to take and what will fit where. The consultant will measure furniture, carpets, drapes, etc., and even offer decorating advice. Maybe your expensive living room drapes can be cut down and reused in your new bedroom and the extra panels made into a bedspread.

If no such service is offered, you will have to do these things yourself. The facility should be able to provide measurements of the rooms in your new residence so you can figure out ahead of time what furniture will fit. Don't forget to get ceiling heights if you have any tall pieces of furniture.

There are several things to consider when deciding what furniture to take with you:

- Function
- Size
- Comfort
- Safety
- Sentimental value

First decide which pieces you are so attached to that you can't imagine parting with them. Then consider whether those pieces will physically fit in your new space and how functional or useful they will be. When considering function, look for pieces that have shelf, drawer, or cabinet space for storage and versatile pieces that may be used in a variety of ways.

Instead of an end table next to a sofa, use a small chest of drawers for added storage. A tilt-top table takes up little space placed upright in a corner, but can be set up easily for card games. A drop-leaf table against a wall can be opened up for special dining occasions.

You can't take everything with you, and some sacrifices are inevitable, but think creatively and you may find some new uses for things. Grandma's trunk now at the foot of your bed may be perfect as your new coffee table while providing extra storage. Remove the mirror from your dresser and use the chest of drawers as an entrance hall table or a server in the dining area.

Consider the comfort, durability, and safety of each piece of furniture. If you're helping a parent move, remember that what you consider comfortable, such as a soft down sofa, is not comfortable for an older person. Chairs and sofas that are high, have firm cushions, and have arms for support are easier for an elderly person to get up from. Remember, also, that elderly people often lean on tables as they rise from chairs, so tables should be sturdy and stable. Pedestal tables are more accommodating to wheelchairs and walkers than tables with legs.

This is the time to part with that carved-back Victorian chair that no one sits in, Grandma's rocking chair with its long rockers that you keep tripping over, the glass coffee table with its sharp edges, and pieces that could be safety hazards because they are too delicate or rickety.

You'll probably find that some things are easy to let go of because you never really liked them anyway, but that you grieve over parting with other things. If you can give those things that you are sentimental about to a child, relative, or friend who will appreciate the gift, you can turn your grief into someone else's joy. Think of it as passing on your things rather than parting with them.

Be sure to tell the person receiving the gift why the item was important to you and write any known history of the item on a card that can be saved for future reference. Include dates, names, and places. Your granddaughter may love the little footstool that she always sits on at your house, but one day she will really appreciate knowing that your father hand-carved that stool for your fifth birthday in 1905 when you lived on a farm in Minnesota.

By now you should have a pretty good idea of what furniture and other things you will be moving to your new home; what, if anything, you plan to sell; and what you want to give away. This is a good time to send out anything you plan to take that needs repair, refinishing, cleaning, or reupholstery. Time it so that these items can be delivered to your new residence if you are moving in the same town. If you're moving out of town, be sure to allow plenty of time so that items can be delivered back to you before the movers arrive.

LABELING THINGS

The next step is to begin labeling things. Go to an office supply store and buy stickers in three different colors. The stickers should be large enough to write on, and the colors should be bright and easily distinguishable from each other. Avoid confusion by making several master index cards—one for each room. Place one of each colored sticker on an index card and write on the sticker or on the card next to the sticker which category you have assigned to that color. Example:

- Pink = move
- Green = give away
- Yellow = sell

Take one room at a time and place stickers on furniture, lamps, paintings, rugs, etc. As you place stickers on items to be moved, write on the sticker which room they will be moved to in your new home (bedroom #1, bedroom #2, living room, kitchen, bath). If you don't know where something will be placed, leave the sticker blank for now and come back to it later.

DIVIDING THINGS

There are many different approaches to dividing things among children. Which approach you take depends on how many things you have to give away, how many children you have, and whether they live nearby. However you proceed, it's best to start by separating those items that for one reason or another you have always planned to give to certain people and writing their names on the appropriate sticker.

If possible, have those people pick up their items. If you have decided to give your best friend the plant stand she has always admired, letting it sit around with her name on it may just invite jealousy and squabbling among family members. Such quarreling is stressful and dampens the spirit of giving.

If your children are likely to fight over your things or if they live too far away, you may prefer to make the decision of who gets what. Write the name of the recipient on the sticker and ask each child to arrange shipping.

If your children live nearby, the ideal situation is to invite them over for a "moving party." Make it a festive occasion, maybe a potluck supper with each child bringing a different dish. Let them have time to look over the items marked with giveaway stickers. Then after dinner have the children draw numbers out of a bowl, and in that order begin selecting what they want.

Ask the children to write their names on the stickers as they select items. Have a pad and pen handy for someone to make a master list of who has chosen what so there won't be any confusion later if stickers come off or are switched. Whatever the children cannot take with them that night should be picked up as soon as possible.

Now you're ready for the movers, who can easily identify the items to be moved by the brightly colored stickers. You can also use the stickers to identify boxes and the room they will be moved to, but don't forget to write on each box a number and a list of its contents. Keep a master list of the boxes by number and contents. If a box is lost you can refer to the master list to determine what is missing.

If you have hired someone to have an estate sale after you've moved, that person can deal with everything left behind, and you can focus your energy on getting settled in your new residence. Moving out is just half of the process; now you have to move in!

MOVING IN

Don't expect everything to be perfect overnight, but recognize the importance of getting settled as quickly as possible. Whether you are moving or you are helping an elderly family member move, remember that older people have less tolerance for confusion. If possible, the person moving should spend the first night or two in a guest room at the facility or with a family member until the new residence is ready for occupancy.

If you're helping Mom move, stay and unpack boxes and help organize things, but let her decide where things go. You may be trying to minimize confusion by putting everything away, but imagine how confusing it would be if someone arranged all of your things in closets, cabinets, and shelves without you knowing where they were. You would feel disoriented and not in control of your own life.

We've already discussed the need for emotional security and the importance of making the new residence look and feel like home, but it's even more important to consider physical safety. In the same way that parents of young children take measures to "child-proof" their home, elderly residents should take measures to make their home "senior friendly" and safe.

CREATING A SENIOR-FRIENDLY ENVIRONMENT

To understand what steps can be taken to make an environment safe for the elderly, let's first consider just a few of the physiological changes of the aging process that necessitate these measures:

- Memory loss/confusion
- Loss of muscle tone and strength
- Bones become brittle and break easily
- Loss of vision
- Loss of hearing
- Decreased circulation (causes extremities to feel cold)
- Increased frequency of urination
- Constipation
- Thinning of the skin causes easy bruising

Many elderly people have already figured out ways to accommodate their living environment to their aging body, but their children may not have given much thought to this. Take for instance bladder and bowel problems. If a person has diarrhea caused by laxatives taken to relieve constipation, or if he or she urinates frequently, the result is frequent and often hurried trips to the bathroom.

Not only should the bed be close to the bathroom door, but the pathway leading to the bathroom from the bedroom and from other rooms should be unobstructed by furniture, electrical cords, and sharp angles. Tripping while hurrying to the bathroom could cause falls and broken bones.

The bathroom itself needs to be safe. It's best to carpet hard floor surfaces such as tile that are damaging to brittle bones in case of falls. Tile floors also become very slippery when wet. Be sure tubs and showers have grab bars and nonslip appliqués. The installation of raised toilet seats eases the task of getting up from a low seated position, which becomes more difficult as joints stiffen and muscles weaken.

Medicine cabinets should be well-lit so that medicine labels can be read easily, and night lights should be installed in bathrooms, as well as bedrooms and hallways.

Burns from scalding water can be a problem for the elderly. Because poor circulation causes extremities to feel cold, bath water may be hotter than it is perceived to be when tested with fingers or toes. Scalding accidents can be prevented by lowering the hot water temperature or installing faucets with a special temperature limit feature.

Bathroom heaters should be located in ceilings or high on the wall to prevent clothing or towels from catching on fire.

Bedrooms and bathrooms in senior residential facilities should be equipped with emergency call systems. Be sure the call button or cord is operating and easily visible.

Kitchens are another common site of accidents and injuries. Again, hard floor surfaces should be avoided. Linoleum or wood floors are better than tile or marble, which are not only hard, but slippery when wet. All kitchens should have smoke detectors, but check the battery when you move in and again at frequent intervals. It's not uncommon for the elderly to forget a pot on the stove or a dish in the oven.

When setting up a residence it's important to give careful consideration to where things are stored. Think about which things are used most frequently and place them within easy reach in the most accessible spots. Inaccessible areas include high shelves that require stretching or step stools to reach and low cabinets that require bending and stooping to reach. Also avoid placing important items in dark corners of closets or cabinets where visibility is difficult.

Lighting is another important consideration. Remember that it takes two to three times more light for the aged eye to see. Counter lights installed under kitchen cabinets are helpful, but good closet lighting is essential. Lights that go on automatically when the door is opened are best, but if you have lights that operate with a pull cord, make sure the cord is long enough. A brightly colored ribbon tied to the end of the cord will make it easier to find in the dark.

Place lamps at strategic spots for good direct lighting for reading, sewing, card playing, etc. Adjustable lamps are ideal in such locations. Other lighting should be bright but indirect to avoid glare. Glare significantly reduces visual acuity.

Most people think about esthetics, convenience, and the best use of space when placing furniture, but frequently forget safety concerns. Cataracts, glaucoma, and macular degeneration are just a few common eyesight problems that cause cloudy or blurred vision or loss of peripheral vision in the elderly. Furniture should be arranged to allow clear, wide pathways from one area to another. Sharp edges and protrusions not easily seen can cause broken bones and severe damage to thin skin.

Don't forget to take vision and hearing problems into account when setting up comfortable seating arrangements for television watching. Be sure telephones are installed in convenient locations where they can be heard and reached easily.

Throw rugs or area rugs should be avoided, but if you do have them, tape down edges securely with double-faced adhesive carpet tape. Either tape down electrical cords or run the cords under rugs.

Other senior-friendly features include large-calibrated thermostats, light switches installed lower than normal, and electrical outlets installed one to two feet above floor level. Lever-type handles are easier for arthritic hands to operate than knobs that require a gripping and twisting motion.

CHECKLIST

MOVING OUT

_____ Organize things you plan to take:

_____ photographs

_____ letters

_____ books

_____ clothes

_____ files and records:

_____ births/deaths

_____ marriage/divorce

_____ citizenship/passport

_____ marriage

_____ will

_____ financial

_____ taxes

_____ legal

_____ medical

_____ insurance (life, health, property, burial)

_____ Social Security

_____ Medicare and Medicaid

_____ automobile

_____ real estate

_____ Throw away junk and clutter

_____ Give things away to:

_____ children

_____ family members

_____ friends

_____ donations

_____ Sell items:

_____   garage sale

_____   estate sale

_____   antique/consignment/resale shop

_____ Hire movers:

_____   check references

_____   check insurance coverage

_____   call Better Business Bureau

_____ Fill out change of address form at post office

_____ Notify others of address change:

_____   magazines

_____   newspapers

_____   credit card companies

_____   department stores

_____   doctors

_____   Social Security

_____   Medicare/Medicaid

_____   insurance

_____   bank (order new checks)

_____   other financial institutions

_____   passport agency

_____   driver's license bureau

_____   voter registration office

_____ Mail moving announcement to friends and family

_____ Order new stationery

_____ Cancel services and get deposits refunded:

_____	gas	_____	water delivery
_____	electricity	_____	pest control
_____	water	_____	yard service

_____ cable television

_____ Arrange for new services (if necessary):

_____ gas	_____ telephone
_____ electricity	_____ cable television
_____ water	

_____ If moving out of town, visit ahead:

_____ open bank account

_____ get safety-deposit box

_____ apply for new driver's license

_____ open charge accounts

_____ apply for grocery check cashing card

_____ In choosing furnishings to take, consider:

_____ function	_____ safety
_____ size	_____ sentimental value
_____ comfort	

_____ Send out things for:

_____ repair	_____ reupholstery
_____ cleaning	_____ refinishing

_____ Label items with colored stickers:

_____ move (which room)

_____ give away

_____ sell

_____ Label boxes:

_____ room it will be moved to

_____ number

_____ list of contents

_____ make master list (number and contents)

MOVING IN

_____ Check residence for safety:

_____ safe furniture placement

_____ clear path to bathroom

_____ tape down throw rugs

_____ carpet slippery or hard bathroom floor surfaces

_____ nonslip appliqués in tubs and showers

_____ grab bars in tubs and showers

_____ emergency response system in bedrooms and baths in working order

_____ well-lit medicine cabinet

_____ raised toilet seats

_____ night lights in baths, bedrooms, hallways

_____ lower temperature of hot water heater

_____ faucets with temperature limit button

_____ space heaters out of way in ceilings or walls

_____ smoke detectors in working order

_____ Check for other senior-friendly features:

_____ kitchen counter lighting under cabinets

_____ good reading lamps in strategic locations

_____ telephones in convenient locations

_____ everyday items stored within easy reach

_____ good closet lighting

_____ lever handles

_____ large-calibrated thermostats

_____ light switches placed lower

_____ electrical outlets placed higher

APPENDICES

Organizations That Provide Services and Information

Caregiver Support

Children of Aging Parents
1609 Woodbourne Road
Suite 302A
Levittown, PA 19057
215-945-6900
800-227-7294

Nonprofit organization founded to offer support to children of aging parents, with the focus on caregiving.

- Maintains a resource and referral file. Assists in developing caregiver support groups nationally.
- Offers individual peer counseling in person and by phone.

Family Caregiver Alliance
425 Bush Street
Suite 500
San Francisco, CA 94108
415-434-3388

- Provides information on caring for people with adult-onset brain disorders (Alzheimer's, stroke, Parkinson's).

- Research specialists can help locate services for caregivers around the country.

National Family Caregivers Association
9621 East Bexhill Drive
Kensington, MD 20895-3104
301-942-6430
301-942-2302 (fax)
800-896-3650

- Call 24-hour toll-free helpline for assistance to caregivers around the country.
- Provides information on caregiving and referrals to support groups.

Well Spouse Foundation
610 Lexington Avenue
Suite 814
New York, NY 10022
212-644-1241
212-644-1338 (fax)
800-838-0879

A support network for the well spouses of chronically ill patients. Provides referrals to local support groups and personal outreach to individuals through letters and phone calls.

Consumer Information

National Consumers League
1701 K Street, N.W.
Suite 1200
Washington, DC 20006
202-835-3323

A private nonprofit consumer advocacy organization that distributes information and materials on a wide range of consumer topics. Call for list of publications for sale, including consumer guides to life-care communities, hospice care, and home-health care.

United States Federal Trade Commission
Pennsylvania Avenue at Sixth Street, N.W.
Washington, DC 20580
202-326-2222
202-326-2502 (TTY)

Call or write for list of consumer education and protection publications.

Death and Dying

Choice in Dying
200 Varick Street
New York, NY 10014
212-366-5540

- Call or write for free copies of living will and health-care proxy for each state.
- Offers counseling service.
- Sells books and videos on death and dying.

National Hospice Organization
1901 N. Moore Street
Suite 901
Arlington, VA 22209
703-243-5900
800-658-8898

National organization founded in 1978, dedicated to educating the public and health-care organizations about hospice care. Call toll-free hospice helpline to locate a hospice program near you or your family member.

Insurance

A.M. Best and Co.
Ambest Road
Oldwick, NJ 08858
908-439-2200
908-439-3296 (fax)
800-424-2378

Private company that publishes *Best's Insurance Reports*, which rates insurance companies based on their financial strength.

Health Insurance Association of America
555 Thirteenth Street, N.W.
Suite 600 East
Washington, DC 20004-1109

• Write for free publications on health insurance.
• Write for free listing by state of insurance companies that sell long-term-care insurance.

National Association of Insurance Commissioners
120 W. Twelfth Street
Suite 1100
Kansas City, MO 64105-1925
816-374-7259
816-471-7004 (fax)

The organization of insurance regulators from the fifty states, the District of Columbia, and the four U.S. territories.

Call or write for single free copy of: *A Shopper's Guide to Long-Term-Care Insurance, A Shopper's Guide to Cancer Insurance, Guide to Health Insurance for People with Medicare*

National Insurance Consumer Helpline
800-942-4242

Answers questions, makes referrals, distributes free educational material on life, health, auto, home, and business insurance.

United Seniors Health Cooperative
1331 H Street, N.W.
Suite 500
Washington, DC 20005-4706
202-393-6222
202-783-0588 (fax)

Provides publications on Medicare, Medigap, and long-term-care insurance.

Legal

American Bar Association
Commission on Legal Problems of the Elderly
740 Fifteenth Street, N.W.
Washington, DC 20005
202-662-8690

Call or write for list of publications.

Legal Counsel for the Elderly, Inc.
601 E Street, N.W.
Washington, DC 20049
202-434-2120

An AARP-sponsored national support center specializing in the delivery of legal services to older persons. Programs focus on the poor and disabled, but some services are provided to all older people. Call or write for list of publications and services.

National Academy of Elder Law Attorneys
1604 North Country Club Road
Tucson, AZ 85716
520-881-4005

Sells a national directory of elder-law attorneys screened by the academy.

Medicare/Medicaid

Medicare Hotline
800-638-6833

Call 8:00 A.M. to 8:00 P.M. (EST) with questions about Medicare coverage.

Social Security Administration
Washington, DC 20402
800-772-1213

- Call for free copy of *Your Medicare Handbook* and other Social Security publications.
- Call with questions on Social Security and Medicare enrollment and eligibility.

U.S. Department of Health and Human Services
Office of Inspector General
200 Independence Avenue, S.W.
Washington, DC 20201
800-368-5779

Call HOTLINE (800-269-0271) to report Medicare-Medicaid fraud and abuse.

Nursing Homes

American Health Care Association
1201 L Street, N.W.
Washington, DC 20005
202-842-4444

A national trade organization of health-care providers. Call or write for free copy of *Thinking About a Nursing Home*.

Foundation Aiding the Elderly
P.O. Box 254849
Sacramento, CA 95865-4849
916-481-8558

A grassroots organization working for nursing home reform. Provides information on reporting nursing home abuse and neglect and referrals on various senior issues.

National Citizens Coalition for Nursing Home Reform
1424 Sixteenth Street, N.W.
Suite 202
Washington, DC 20036
202-332-2275

Clearinghouse for information on nursing home and board care issues.

Nursing Home Information Service
National Council of Senior Citizens
1331 F Street, N.W.
Washington, DC 20004-1171
202-347-8800

Provides information and referrals on nursing homes, as well as other types of housing for the elderly.

Residential Facilities

American Association of Homes and Services for the Aging
901 E Street, N.W.
Suite 500
Washington, DC 20004-2037
202-783-2242
202-783-2255 (fax)

The national trade organization of nonprofit providers of housing, health, community, and related services to the elderly. Call or write for list of consumer publications for sale, including: *The Continuing Care Retirement Community: A Guidebook for Consumers; The Consumers' Directory of Continuing Care Retirement Communities.*

Continuing Care Accreditation Commission
901 E Street, N.W.
Suite 500
Washington, DC 20004-2037
202-783-2242

Independent commission established by the American Association of Homes and Services for the Aging to evaluate and accredit both nonprofit and for-profit continuing-care retirement communities. Send stamped, self-addressed, business-size envelope for a free list of accredited continuing-care retirement communities.

National Institute of Senior Housing
409 Third Street, S.W.
Washington, DC 20024
202-479-1200

Clearinghouse for information about housing options for older adults.

Senior Issues and Services

American Association of Retired Persons (AARP)
601 E Street, N.W.
Washington, DC 20049
202-434-6030
800-424-3410

A nonprofit membership organization that offers a wide range of programs and services for people age fifty or older.

American Society on Aging
833 Market Street
Suite 511
San Francisco, CA 94103-1824
415-974-9600
415-974-0300 (fax)

Publishes a quarterly journal, *Generations*, and a bimonthly newspaper, *Aging Today*, available by subscription.

Association of Retired Americans
9102 N. Meridian Street
Suite 405
Indianapolis, IN 46260-1826
317-571-6888
317-571-6895 (fax)
800-806-6160

A nonprofit membership organization that provides services at a discount to American seniors.

Eldercare Locator
800-677-1116

A national resource to help consumers identify the most appropriate local organization for information and assistance for seniors. Call

9:00 A.M. to 8:00 P.M. (EST) for information on organizations serving older adults in your area.

National Council on Aging
409 Third Street, S.W.
Washington, DC 20024
202-479-1200
202-479-6674 (TTY)
800-424-9046

National organization of professionals and individual consumers interested in information, ideas, and issues in aging. Call for list of publications for sale.

National Association of Geriatric Care Managers
1604 North Country Club Road
Tucson, AZ 85716
520-881-8008
520-325-7925 (fax)

Call or write for free referral to geriatric care managers in your area. Geriatric care managers assist seniors and their families with long-term care.

APPENDIX B

State Agencies on Aging

Alabama
Commission on Aging
Suite 470
770 Washington Avenue
Montgomery, AL 36130
334-242-5743

Alaska
Division of Senior Services
Department of Administration
P.O. Box 110211
Juneau, AK 99811
907-465-4400

Arizona
Aging and Adult
Administration
1789 W. Jefferson Street
Phoenix, AZ 85007
602-542-4446

Arkansas
Division of Aging and Adult
Services
Department of Human
Services
P.O. Box 1437, Slot 1412
Little Rock, AR 72203
501-682-2441

California
Department of Aging
1600 K Street
Sacramento, CA 95814
916-322-3887

Colorado
Aging and Adult Service
Department of Social Services
110 16th Street, 2nd Floor
Denver, CO 80202
303-620-4147

Connecticut
Elderly Services Division
Department of Social Services
25 Sigourney Street
Hartford, CT 06106
203-424-4925
800-443-9946

Delaware
Division on Aging
Department of Health and
Social Services
256 Chapman Road
Oxford Building Suite 200
Newark, DE 19702

302-453-3820
800-223-9074 (in state only)

District of Columbia
Office on Aging
441 Fourth Street, N.W.
Room 900S
Washington, D.C. 20001
202-724-5626

Florida
Program Office of Aging and
Adult Services
Department of Health and
Rehabilitative Services
1317 Winewood Boulevard
Building 5, Room 200
Tallahassee, FL 32399-0700
904-488-8922

Georgia
Office of Aging
2 Peachtree Street, N.W.
Suite 18-403
Atlanta, GA 30303
404-657-5258

Hawaii
Executive Office on Aging
250 South Hotel Street
Suite 107
Honolulu, HI 96813
808-586-0100

Idaho
Commission on Aging
Room 108, Statehouse
P.O. Box 83720
Boise, ID 83720-0007
208-334-3833

Illinois
Department on Aging
421 East Capitol Avenue
Suite 100
Springfield, IL 62701-1789
217-785-3356
800-252-8966 (in state only)

Indiana
Bureau of Aging
P.O. Box 7083
Indianapolis, IN 46207-7083
317-232-7020
800-545-7763

Iowa
Department of Elder Affairs
200 10th Street
3rd Floor
Des Moines, IA 50309-3609
515-281-5187

Kansas
Department on Aging
Docking State Office Building
150-S
915 SW Harrison
Topeka, KS 66612-1500
913-296-4986

Kentucky
Division of Aging Services
Cabinet for Human Resources
CHR Building 5th Floor W
275 East Main Street
Frankfort, KY 40621
502-564-6930

Louisiana
Office of Elderly Affairs
P.O. Box 80374
Baton Rouge, LA 70898-0374
504-925-1700

Maine
Bureau of Elder and Adult
Services
Department of Human
Services
35 Anthony Avenue
Augusta, ME 04333-0011
207-624-5335

Maryland
Office of Aging
State Office Building
301 West Preston Street
Room 1004
Baltimore, MD 21201
410-225-1102

Massachusetts
Executive Office of Elder
Affairs
1 Ashburton Place, 5th Floor
Boston, MA 02108
617-727-7750
800-882-2003 (in state only)

Michigan
Office of Services to the
Aging
611 W. Ottawa St.
P.O. Box 30026
Lansing, MI 48909
517-373-8230

Minnesota
Board on Aging
444 Lafayette Road
St. Paul, MN 55155-3843
612-296-2770

Mississippi
Division of Aging and Adult
Services
Department of Health and
Human Services
750 North State Street
Jackson, MS 39202
601-359-4929
800-948-3090 (in state only)

Missouri
Division of Aging
Department of Social Services
P.O. Box 1337
615 Howerton Court
Jefferson City, MO 65102-1337
573-751-3082

Montana
Office on Aging
111 Sanders Old SRS
Building
Helena, MT 59620
406-444-4077

Nebraska
Department on Aging
P.O. Box 95044
301 Centennial Mall, South
Lincoln, NE 68509-5044
402-471-2306

Nevada
Division for Aging Services
Department of Human
Resources
340 North 11th Street
Suite 203
Las Vegas, NV 89101
702-486-3545

New Hampshire
Division of Elderly and
Adult Services
115 Pleasant Street
Concord, NH 03301
603-271-4680

New Jersey
Division of Aging
Department of Community
Affairs
CN807 South Broad and
Front Streets
Trenton, NJ 08625-0807
609-984-3951
800-792-8820 (in state only)

New Mexico
State Agency on Aging
228 East Palace Avenue
La Villa Rivera Building
Santa Fe, NM 87501
505-827-7640

New York
Office for Aging
Empire State Plaza
Albany, NY 12223-1251
518-474-5731
800-342-9871 (in state only)

North Carolina
Division of Aging
693 Palmer Drive
Raleigh, NC 27626-0531
919-733-3983

North Dakota
Aging Services
600 South Second Street
Room 1C
Bismarck, ND 58504-5729
701-328-8910
800-755-8521 (in state only)

Ohio
Department of Aging
50 West Broad Street, 9th floor
Columbus, OH 43215-5928
614-466-5500
800-282-1206 (in state only)

Oklahoma
Aging Services Division
312 NE 28th Street
Oklahoma City, OK 73105
405-521-2327

Oregon
Senior and Disabled Services
500 Summer Street NE,
2nd Floor
Salem, OR 97310-1015
503-945-5811
800-232-3020 (in state only)

Pennsylvania
Department of Aging
400 Market Street
Harrisburg, PA 17101-2301
717-783-1550

Rhode Island
Department of Elderly
Affairs
160 Pine Street
Providence, RI 02903-3708
401-277-2880

South Carolina
Division on Aging
202 Arbor Lake Drive
Suite 301
Columbia, SC 29223
803-737-7500

South Dakota
Office of Adult Services and
Aging
700 Governors Drive
Kneip Building
Pierre, SD 57501
605-773-3656

Tennessee
Commission on Aging
Andrew Jackson Building
500 Deaderick Street,
9th Floor
Nashville, TN 37243-0860
615-741-2056

Texas
Department on Aging
4900 North Lamar Blvd.
4th floor
Austin, TX 78751-2316
512-424-6840
800-252-9240 (in state only)

Utah
Division of Aging and Adult
Services
Department of Human
Services
120 North–200 West
Salt Lake City, UT 84103
801-538-3910

Vermont
Aging and Disabilities
103 South Main Street
Waterbury, VT 05671-2301
802-241-2400

Virginia
Department for Aging
700 East Franklin Street
10th Floor
Richmond, VA 23219-2327
804-225-2271
800-552-3402 (in state only)

Washington
Aging and Adult Services
Administration
Department of Social and
Health Services
P.O. Box 45050
Olympia, WA 98504-5050
360-902-7797

West Virginia
Commission on Aging
State Capitol
Charleston, WV 25305
304-558-3317

Wisconsin

Bureau on Aging
Division of Community
Services
217 South Hamilton Street
Suite 300
Madison, WI 53703
608-266-2536

Wyoming

Division on Aging
Hathaway Building,
Room 139
2300 Capitol Avenue
Cheyenne, WY 82002-0480
307-777-7986
800-442-2766 (in state only)

APPENDIX C

Agencies Reponsible for Regulating and/or Licensing Assisted-Living Facilities

Following is an alphabetical listing by state of agencies responsible for regulating and licensing assisted-living facilities. Listed in italics next to each state is the licensing terminology used for assisted-living facilities in that state.

Alabama
(Assisted-Living Facility)
Department of Public Health
Division of Licensure and
Certification
434 Monroe Street
Montgomery, AL 36130-3017
334-261-6520

Alaska
(Assisted-Living Home)
Department of Administration
Division of Senior Services
Assisted Living Licensing
3601 C Street
Anchorage, AK 99503
907-563-5654

Arizona
(Residential-Care Facility)
Department of Health Services
Home and Community Based
1647 East Morten
Phoenix, AZ 85020
602-255-1199

Arkansas
(Long-Term Residential-Care Facility)
Department of Human
Services
Office of Long-Term Care
P.O. Box 8059, Slot 408
Little Rock, AR 72203-8059
501-682-8468

California
(Residential-Care Facility for the Elderly)
Department of Social Services
Community Care Licensing
Division
2400 Glendale Lane
Sacramento, CA 95825
916-574-2346

Colorado
(Personal-Care Boarding Home)
Department of Public Health
and Environment
Health Facilities Division
4300 Cherry Creek Drive
South
Denver, CO 80222-1530
303-692-2800

Connecticut
(Assisted-Living Facility)
Department of Public Health
Health Systems Regulation
410 Capitol Avenue
MS #12HSR
P.O. Box 340308
Hartford, CT 06134-0308
203-509-7400

Delaware
(Assisted-Living Facility)
Department of Health and
Social Services
Health Facility Licensing
and Certification
3 Mill Road
Wilmington, DE 19806
302-577-6666

District of Columbia
(Community Residential Facility)
Department of Consumer
and Regulatory Affairs
Service Facility Regulation
Administration
614 H Street, N.W.
Washington, D.C. 20001
202-727-7226

Florida
(Assisted-Living Facility)
Agency for Health Care
Administration
Assisted-Living Facilities
2727 Mahan Drive
Tallahassee, FL 32308
904-487-2515

Georgia
(Personal-Care Home)
Department of Human
Resources
Office of Regulatory Services
2 Peachtree Street, N.W.
21st Floor
Atlanta, GA 30303-3167
404-657-4076

Hawaii
(Adult Residential-Care Home)
Department of Health
Hospital and Medical Facili-
ties Branch
P.O. Box 3378
Honolulu, HI 96801
808-586-4100

Idaho
(Residential-Care Facility)
Department of Health and
Welfare
Bureau of Facility Standards
450 West State Street
P.O. Box 83720
Boise, ID 83720-0036
208-334-6626

Illinois
(Sheltered-Care Facility)
Department of Public Health
Division of Long-Term-Care
Quality Assurance
525 West Jefferson Street
Springfield, IL 62761
217-782-5180

Indiana
(Residential-Care Facility)
Department of Health
Division of Long-Term-Care
2 North Meridian Street
Indianapolis, IN 46204
317-383-6442

Iowa
(Residential-Care Facility)
Department of Inspections
and Appeals
Division of Health Facilities
Lucas State Office Building,
3rd Floor
Des Moines, IA 50319-0083
515-281-4115

Kansas
(Assisted-Living Facility)
Department of Health and
Environment
Bureau of Adult and Child
Care
900 SW Jackson Street
Suite 1001
Topeka, KS 66612
913-296-1240

Kentucky
(Personal-Care Home)
Cabinet for Human Resources
Office of Inspector General
Division of Licensing and
Regulation
CHR Building, 4th Floor East
275 East Main Street
Frankfort, KY 40621-0001
502-564-2800

Louisiana
(Adult Residential-Care Facility)
Department of Social Services
Licensing Bureau
P.O. Box 3078
Baton Rouge, LA 70821-3078
504-922-0015

Maine
*(Boarding Home and Adult Fos-
ter Home)*
Department of Human Services
Division of Licensing and
Certification
Residential Care Unit
35 Anthony Avenue
Augusta, ME 04333
207-624-5250

Maryland
(Group Senior Assisted Housing)
Office on Aging
Senior Assisted Housing
Division
301 West Preston Street
Baltimore, MD 22101-2375
410-225-1083

Massachusetts
(Assisted-Living Residence)
Executive Office of Elder
Affairs
1 Ashburton Place, 5th Floor
Boston, MA 02108
617-727-7750

Michigan
(Adult Foster-Care Facility)
Department of Social Services
Adult Foster-Care Licensing
235 South Grand Avenue
Suite 1208
Lansing, MI 48909
517-373-8580

Minnesota
(Board and Lodging House with Special Services)
Department of Health
Environmental Health Division
Metro Square Building
P.O. Box 64975
St. Paul, MN 55164-0975
612-215-0870

Mississippi
(Personal-Care Home)
Department of Health
Licensure and Certification
P.O. Box 1700
Jackson, MS 39215-1700
601-354-7300

Missouri
(Residential-Care Facility)
Department of Social Services
Division of Aging
P.O. Box 1337
Jefferson City, MO 65102-1337
573-751-3082

Montana
(Personal-Care Facility)
Department of Public Health
and Human Services
Licensure Bureau
Cogswell Building
P.O. Box 202951
Helena, MT 59620-2951
406-444-2037

Nebraska
(Residential-Care Facility)
Department of Health
Section of Health Facility Licensure and Inspection
P.O. Box 95007
Lincoln, NE 68509-5007
402-471-2949

Nevada
(Residential Facility for Groups)
Division of Health
Bureau of Licensure and
Certification
1550 East College Parkway,
#158
Carson City, NV 89710
702-687-4475

New Hampshire
*(Residential Care Home Facility
and Supported Residential-Care
Facility)*
Bureau of Health Facilities
Administration
Division of Public Health
Services
6 Hazen Drive
Concord, NH 03301-6527
603-271-4592

New Jersey
*(Assisted Living Residence and
Comprehensive Personal Care
Home)*
Department of Health
Division of Health Facilities
Evaluation and Licensing
CN367
Trenton, NJ 08625
609-588-7725

New Mexico
(Assisted-Living Facility)
Department of Health
Licensing and Certification
525 Camino de los Marquez
Suite 2

Santa Fe, NM 87501
505-827-4225

New York
*(Adult Home and Enriched
Housing)*
Department of Social Services
Office of Housing and Adult
Services
40 North Pearl Street
Albany, NY 12243
518-432-2400

North Carolina
(Adult Care Home)
Department of Human
Resources
Division of Facility Services
Group Care Section
P.O. Box 29530
Raleigh, NC 27626-0530
919-733-2342

North Dakota
(Basic Care Facility)
Department of Health
Division of Health Facilities
600 East Boulevard Avenue
Bismarck, ND 58505-0200
701-328-2352

Ohio
(Residential-Care Facility)
Department of Health
Division of Quality Assurance
236 North High Street
P.O. Box 118
Columbus, OH 43266-0118
614-466-7713

Oklahoma
(Residential-Care Home)
Department of Health
Special Health Services
1000 Northeast Tenth Street
Oklahoma City, OK 73117-
1299
405-271-6868

Oregon
(Assisted-Living Facility)
Senior and Disabled Services
Division
500 Summer Street, N.E.
Salem, OR 97310-1015
503-945-5832

Pennsylvania
(Personal-Care Home)
Department of Public Welfare
Office of Social Programs
Division of Personal-
Care Homes
Bertolino Building, 2nd Floor
1401 North Seventh Street
P.O. Box 2675
Harrisburg, PA 17105-2675
717-783-4504

Rhode Island
*(Assisted Living/Residential
Care)*
Department of Health
Division of Facilities
Regulation
3 Capitol Hill
Providence, RI 02908-5097
401-277-2566

South Carolina
*(Community Residential-Care
Facility)*
Department of Health and
Environmental Control
Division of Health Licensing
2600 Bull Street
Columbia, SC 29201
803-737-7202

South Dakota
(Assisted-Living Center)
Department of Health
Office of Health Care
Facilities
Licensure and Certification
445 East Capitol
Pierre, SD 57501-3185
605-773-3364

Tennessee
(Residential Home for the Aged)
Department of Health
Division of Health Care
Facilities
283 Plus Park Boulevard
Nashville, TN 37247-0530
615-367-6308

Texas
(Personal-Care Facility)
Department of Human
Services
Long-Term-Care Division
Licensing Section
8407 Wall Street
Austin, TX 78754
512-834-6697

Utah
(Assisted-Living Facility)
Department of Health
Bureau of Health Facility
Licensure
Box 142853
Salt Lake City, UT 84114-2853
801-538-6152

Vermont
(Residential-Care Home)
Agency of Human Services
Division of Licensing and
Protection
Ladd Hall
103 South Main Street
Waterbury, VT 05671-2306
802-241-2345

Virginia
(Adult-Care Residence)
Department of Social Services
Division of Licensing
Programs
730 East Broad Street
Richmond, VA 23219
804-692-1787

Washington
(Boarding Home)
Department of Health
Boarding Home Licensing
P.O. Box 47852
Olympia, WA 98504-7852
360-705-6652

West Virginia
(Personal-Care Home)
Department of Health and
Human Services
Office of Health Facility
Licensure and Certification
1900 Kanawha Boulevard
East
Building 3, Room 550
Charleston, WV 25305-0430
304-558-0050

Wisconsin
(Community-Based Residential Facility)
Department of Health and
Social Services
Division of Community
Services
Bureau of Regional Operations
1 West Wilson Street,
Room 534
P.O. Box 7851
Madison, WI 53707
608-267-8928

Wyoming
(Assisted-Living Facility)
Department of Health
Office of Health Quality
First Bank Building, 8th Floor
2020 Carey Avenue
Cheyenne, WY 82002
307-777-7123

APPENDIX D

Insurance Departments and Special Insurance Counseling Offices

State departments of insurance are responsible for regulating the insurance industry and providing insurance information to consumers. Call your state's insurance department to find out if a broker or agent is licensed, to get assistance in understanding insurance bills and claims, and to request free printed information on different types of health insurance.

Call the insurance counseling number in your state with questions on Medicare, Medicaid, Medigap, and long-term-care insurance.

All toll-free numbers are for in-state dialing only.

Alabama

Insurance Department
Consumer Services Division
135 South Union Street
Suite 181
Montgomery, AL 36130
334-269-3550

Insurance Counseling
800-243-5463

Alaska

Division of Insurance
Frontier Building
3601 C Street
Suite 1324
Anchorage, AL 99503-5948
907-269-7900

Insurance Counseling
907-562-7249
800-478-6065

Arizona

Department of Insurance
Consumer Assistance Division
2910 North 44th Street
Suite 210
Phoenix, AZ 85018
602-912-8444
800-325-2548

Insurance Counseling
602-542-6595
800-432-4040

Arkansas

Insurance Department
1200 West Third Street
Little Rock, AR 72201
501-371-2600
800-852-5494

Insurance Counseling
501-371-2780
800-852-5494

California

Department of Insurance
Consumer Services Division
300 South Spring Street
Los Angeles, CA 90013
213-897-8921
800-927-4357

Insurance Counseling
916-323-7315
800-927-4357

Colorado

Division of Insurance
1560 Broadway

Suite 850
Denver, CO 80202
303-894-7499

Insurance Counseling
800-544-9181

Connecticut

Insurance Department
P.O. Box 816
Hartford, CT 06142-0816
203-297-3800

Insurance Counseling
800-443-9946

Delaware

Insurance Department
841 Silver Lake Boulevard
P.O. Box 7007
Dover, DE 19903-1507
302-739-4251
800-282-8611

Insurance Counseling
800-336-9500

District of Columbia

Insurance Department
Consumer Services Bureau
441 Fourth Street, N.W.
Washington, DC 20001
202-727-8000

Insurance Counseling
202-994-7463

Florida
Department of Insurance
200 East Gaines Street
Tallahassee, FL 32399-0300
904-922-3100
800-342-2962

Insurance Counseling
904-414-2060

Georgia
Insurance Department
Consumer Services Division
Room 716 West Tower
2 Martin Luther
King, Jr. Drive
Atlanta, GA 30334
404-656-2056

Insurance Counseling
800-669-8387

Hawaii
Division of Insurance
P.O. Box 3614
Honolulu, HI 96811
808-586-2790

Insurance Counseling
808-586-0100

Idaho
Department of Insurance
Consumer Assistance
P.O. Box 83720
Boise, ID 83720-0043
208-334-2250
800-721-3272

Insurance Counseling
208-334-4350

Illinois
Department of Insurance
Consumer Services
320 West Washington Street
Springfield, IL 62767
217-782-4515

Insurance Counseling
800-548-9034

Indiana
Department of Insurance
311 West Washington Street
Suite 300
Indianapolis, IN 46204-2787
317-232-2395
800-622-4461

Insurance Counseling
800-452-4800

Iowa
Insurance Division
Lucas State Office Building
6th Floor
Des Moines, IA 50319
515-281-5705

Insurance Counseling
800-351-4664

Kansas
Insurance Department
Consumer Assistance Division

420 Southwest 9th Street
Topeka, KS 66612
913-296-3071
800-432-2484

Insurance Counseling
800-860-5260

Kentucky
Department of Insurance
P.O. Box 517
Frankfort, KY 40602
502-564-3630

Insurance Counseling
800-372-2973

Louisiana
Department of Insurance
Consumer Affairs Department
P.O. Box 94214
Baton Rouge, LA 70804-9214
504-342-5900
800-259-5300

Insurance Counseling
504-342-5301
800-259-5301

Maine
Bureau of Insurance
Consumer Division
24 State House Station
Augusta, ME 04333
207-624-8475
800-300-5000

Insurance Counseling
800-750-5353

Maryland
Insurance Administration
501 St. Paul Place
Baltimore, MD 21202
410-333-3288
800-492-6116

Insurance Counseling
800-243-3425

Massachusetts
Insurance Division
Consumer Services Section
470 Atlantic Avenue
Boston, MA 02210
617-521-7777

Insurance Counseling
800-882-2003

Michigan
Insurance Bureau
P.O. Box 30220
Lansing, MI 48909
517-373-0240

Insurance Counseling
517-373-8230

Minnesota
Insurance Department
133 East Seventh Street
St. Paul, MN 55101-2362
612-296-4026

Insurance Counseling
800-882-6262

Mississippi
Insurance Department
Consumer Assistance Division
P.O. Box 79
Jackson, MS 39205
601-359-3569

Insurance Counseling
800-948-3090

Missouri
Department of Insurance
Consumer Services
P.O. Box 690
Jefferson City, MO
65102-0690
314-751-2640
800-726-7390

Insurance Counseling
800-390-3330

Montana
Insurance Department
P.O. Box 4009
Helena, MT 59601
406-444-2040

Insurance Counseling
800-332-2272

Nebraska
Insurance Department
941 "O" Street
Suite 400
Lincoln, NE 68508
402-471-2201

Insurance Counseling
402-471-4506

Nevada
Division of Insurance
1665 Hot Springs Road
Suite 152
Carson City, NV 89710
702-687-4270

Insurance Counseling
800-307-4444

New Hampshire
Insurance Department
169 Manchester Street
Concord, NH 03301
603-271-2261
800-852-3416

Insurance Counseling
603-271-4642
800-852-3388

New Jersey
Department of Insurance
20 West State Street
CN 325
Trenton, NJ 08625
609-292-5363

Insurance Counseling
800-792-8820

New Mexico
Insurance Department
P.O. Drawer 1269
Santa Fe, NM 87504-1269
505-827-4500

Insurance Counseling
800-432-2080

New York
Insurance Department
160 West Broadway
New York, NY 10013
212-602-0203

Insurance Counseling
212-869-3850
800-333-4114

North Carolina
Insurance Department
Consumer Division
P.O. Box 26387
Raleigh, NC 27611
919-733-2032
800-662-7777

Insurance Counseling
919-733-0111
800-443-9354

North Dakota
Insurance Department
600 East Boulevard
5th Floor
Bismarck, ND 58505
701-328-2440
800-247-0560

Insurance Counseling
800-247-0560

Ohio
Department of Insurance
Consumer Services Division
2100 Stella Court
Columbus, OH 43215-1067
614-644-2673
800-686-1526

Insurance Counsling
800-686-1578

Oklahoma
Insurance Department
1901 N. Walnut Street
Oklahoma City, OK 73152-3408
405-521-6628

Insurance Counseling
405-521-6628

Oregon
Insurance Department
350 Winter Street, N.E.
Room 470
Salem, OR 97310
503-378-4484
800-722-4134

Insurance Counseling
800-722-4134

Pennsylvania
Insurance Department
Consumer Services Bureau
1321 Strawberry Square
Harrisburg, PA 17120
717-787-2317

Insurance Counseling
800-783-7067

Rhode Island
Insurance Division
233 Richmond Street
Suite 233
Providence, RI 02903-4233
401-277-2223

Insurance Counseling
800-322-2880

South Carolina
Department of Insurance
Consumer Services Section
P.O. Box 100105
Columbia, SC 29202-3105
803-737-6180
800-768-3467

Insurance Counseling
800-868-9095

South Dakota
Department of Insurance
500 E. Capitol Avenue
Pierre, SD 57501-5070
605-773-3563

Insurance Counseling
605-773-3656

Tennessee
Department of Insurance
500 James Robertson
Parkway

4th Floor
Nashville, TN 37243
615-741-4955
800-525-2816

Insurance Counseling
800-525-2816

Texas
Department of Insurance
P.O. Box 149091
Austin, TX 78714-9091
512-463-6500
800-252-3439

Insurance Counseling
800-252-3439

Utah
Insurance Department
Consumer Services Division
3110 State Office Building
Salt Lake City, UT 84114-6901
801-538-3805
800-439-3805

Insurance Counseling
801-538-3910
800-606-0608

Vermont
Department of Insurance
State Office Building
89 Main Street, Drawer 20
Montpelier, VT 05620-3101
802-828-3302

Insurance Counseling
802-828-3302

Virginia
Bureau of Insurance
Consumer Services Division
P.O. Box 1157
Richmond, VA 23209
804-371-9741
800-552-8945

Insurance Counseling
800-552-3402

Washington
Insurance Department
Consumer Advocacy and
Outreach
P.O. Box 40256
Olympia, WA 98504-0256
360-753-3613
800-562-6900

Insurance Counseling
360-407-3083
800-397-4422

West Virginia
Insurance Department
Consumer Service Division
P.O. Box 50540
Charleston, WV 25305-0540
304-558-3386
800-642-9004

Insurance Counseling
304-558-3317

Wisconsin
Insurance Department
P.O. Box 7873
Madison, WI 53707
608-266-0103
800-236-8517

Insurance Counseling
800-242-1060

Wyoming
Insurance Department
122 West 25th Street
Cheyenne, WY 82002
307-777-7401
800-438-5768

Insurance Counseling
800-438-5768

Glossary

Accepting Assignment: Refers to the agreement by health-care providers who choose to participate in the Medicare program that they will accept the amount that Medicare approves as payment for services rendered. Medicare assigns or pays 80 percent of the approved amount directly to the provider. The Medicare beneficiary is responsible for the remaining 20 percent coinsurance charge.

Accreditation: A stamp of approval or recognition given by a private organization to indicate that the accredited facility meets certain standards set forth by the organization. Accreditation does not indicate fulfillment of legal requirements necessary to operate under state law.

Activities of Daily Living (ADLs): Activities such as eating, bathing, dressing, grooming, going to the toilet, and transferring to and from chair or bed. Whether a person can perform these functions independently or whether he or she needs assistance with these functions determines the appropriate level of care in a residential facility.

Acute Care: The type of medical care provided under the supervision of a physician in a hospital, as opposed to skilled nursing and intermediate care that can be provided in a nursing facility.

Administrator: A person licensed by the state to manage the day-to-day operations of a skilled-nursing facility.

Adult Day Care: Care provided for elderly and disabled adults for a period of less than twenty-four hours. The type of care usually includes supervision, medication, meals, and social activities. The concept is the same as child day care.

Advance Directives: Refers to directions made in advance by individuals regarding their medical treatment in the event they become incapacitated. (See **Living Will** and **Durable Power of Attorney for Health Care**.)

Age-in-Place: A term that refers to a senior's ability to remain in a facility or environment as he or she ages and requires varying degrees of care. A facility that provides different levels of care, from independent living to assisted living to skilled-nursing care, allows a person to "age in place" without having to move from that facility.

Ageism: Prejudice or discrimination against older people.

All-Inclusive Contract: See **Extensive Contract**.

Ambulatory: The term means "able to walk." Some residential facilities have an entrance requirement that residents be ambulatory, which usually means that they are able to walk without the aid of a walker.

Ambulatory Care: See **Outpatient Care**.

Amenities: Extra features, services, or conveniences provided by a facility to make the facility more attractive to residents.

Americans with Disabilities Act (ADA): Civil rights legislation enacted by Congress on July 26, 1990, that protects people with physical and mental disabilities from discrimination. The act prohibits discrimination in employment and by state and local government. It provides for access to buses and trains and to privately operated public accommodations. It requires that federally funded television public service announcements be closed-captioned for the hearing-impaired and that telephone companies provide continuous voice transmission relay services for the hearing- and speech-impaired.

Area Agency on Aging: Each state has an agency on aging. Within the state are various area agencies on aging that serve as advocates for older persons at local levels. These federally and state-funded agencies administer local and regional programs for seniors aged sixty and older. The area agency on aging in your community can provide information on a variety of services for seniors such as adult day care, home-health services, transportation, home-delivered meals, legal assistance, home-health care, and housing options.

Assets: The things you own that have value, such as property, cars, insurance policies, jewelry, cash, savings account, and stocks and bonds. The value of your assets (with some exclusions) and the amount of your income determine your eligibility for Medicaid.

Assignment: See **Accepting Assignment.**

Assisted Living: Refers to a level of care that provides seniors with assistance with activities of daily living, such as eating, bathing, grooming, going to the toilet, and walking and moving to and from chair and bed. Assisted living is for seniors who are not able to live independently, but who do not need to live in a nursing home. The concept of assisted living is referred to by other names in different states. (See Appendix C.)

Assistive Devices: Things designed to help disabled people perform everyday activities, such as walkers, wheelchairs, hearing aids, prostheses, magnifiers, easy-grip scissors, recording equipment, and talking clocks.

Audiologist: A professional who tests and treats people with hearing defects. An audiologist is not a physician.

Audited: Refers to a financial statement prepared by a certified public accountant (CPA) in accordance with Generally Accepted Accounting Procedures.

Balance Sheet: A listing of the assets and liabilities of an individual or a company during a particular accounting period.

Beneficiary: A person who receives insurance benefits or payments.

Benefit Period: The maximum period of time that an insurance company will pay certain benefits. For example, a long-term-care insurance policy might pay for a one-year, five-year, or lifetime nursing home stay. You pay more for a longer benefit period.

Campus Setting: Refers to a residential or business community where a number of buildings are spread out on an expanse of grounds owned by the community. For example, a senior residential facility in a campus setting might include individual cottages for independent living in one area, two apartment buildings for assisted living in another, and a separate nursing facility elsewhere on the grounds. Senior residential facilities in a noncampus setting might include all levels of care in a single building or in several buildings clustered together.

Capitation: A method of reimbursing health-care providers based on a fixed dollar amount per person per month, as opposed to the traditional fee-for-service system.

Cardiologist: A physician who specializes in the diagnosis and treatment of heart problems.

Certification: The process by which hospitals and nursing facilities receive approval from the state to participate in the Medicare or Medicaid program, thus being able to receive reimbursement from the government for services provided to Medicare or Medicaid patients.

Certified Public Accountant (CPA): A public accountant certified as having passed an examination.

Chiropractor: A person trained and licensed to use physical manipulation and adjustment of the spine and joints as a means of treating disease.

Coinsurance: A copayment made by the insured for his or her share of the cost of a covered service. The insurer (such as Medicare or a private insurance company) pays a certain portion of a covered service, and the insured pays the remainder. Coinsurance may be a percent of the total charge or a flat dollar amount.

Common Areas: In condominium and cooperative facilities residents are responsible for maintaining their individual residential unit, but places such as hallways, stairways, lobbies, elevators, grounds, and other areas that are used by all residents are called *common areas.* Residents pay a monthly fee to cover their share of the operating and maintenance costs for these common areas.

Compilation: Refers to a financial report prepared with information collected and assembled, but not verified, by the preparer.

Condominium: A form of ownership where a resident has title to his or her residential unit and an undivided interest in the common areas (such as the land, halls, stairs, elevators, parking area, and lobby) of a residential facility or community. The resident buys an apartment or other type of residential unit and pays a monthly fee to cover his share of the operating and maintenance costs for the common areas.

Construction Deposit: A partial payment made to reserve a space in a facility that is under construction.

Continuing-Care Accreditation Commission: An independent, private commission formed in 1985 to establish standards for continuing care retirement communities. Communities that meet the standards set forth by the commission receive accreditation. Accreditation is simply the commission's stamp of approval and does not indicate the fulfillment of any legal requirements.

Continuing-Care Retirement Community (CCRC): A type of senior residential facility that provides a continuum of care that includes housing, services, and health care to residents on a contractual basis. The contract guarantees these services (or at least access to these services) for a minimum of one year, but usually for the lifetime of the resident. The most common type of contract is an entrance-fee contract where the resident pays a lump-sum fee to enter the facility plus a monthly fee. In some CCRCs, however, residents buy a condominium or cooperative (instead of paying an entrance fee) and pay monthly maintenance fees. A few CCRCs operate on the basis of a monthly-fee contract where monthly fees are considerably higher than with the other two types of contracts, but residents do not make a substantial initial investment.

Contract: A legally binding agreement between two or more parties.

Cooperative: A form of ownership where a resident does not own an apartment outright but owns shares in a corporation, partnership, or trust that holds title to the entire building. Ownership of those shares allows the resident to *occupy* (not own) a specific unit in the building. (Note that a condominium owner actually *owns* title to a specific unit.) Each resident also pays a monthly fee to cover his or her share of the operating and maintenance costs of the common areas (such as hallways, elevators, grounds, and stairways), plus his or her share of the mortgage and taxes for the entire property.

Copayment: See **Coinsurance.**

Cueing: The use of memory aids, verbal reminders, and design elements to help people with memory loss maintain their daily routines.

Custodial Nursing Care: Room, board, and basic supervision and assistance with personal needs (eating, bathing, dressing, grooming, and mobility) provided by unlicensed personnel. Does not include medical assistance.

Death Benefits: An insurance benefit that provides that if the insured dies, the insurance company will reimburse that person's estate or beneficiary all of the premiums paid over the years, minus the amount of any benefits that the insurance company paid out on the policy.

Declining Balance Refund: The amount to be refunded is determined on a declining scale basis with a certain amount subtracted at given time periods. For example, two percent of a deposit is subtracted for each month that a resident remains at a facility.

Deductible: A specified amount that a person must pay before insurance coverage begins. The higher the deductible, the lower the premium should be.

Depression: Prolonged feelings of sadness and hopelessness that if left untreated can lead to suicide. Symptoms may include listlessness, anxiety, difficulty sleeping, weight loss or gain, inability to cope, and a general loss of interest in life. Depression may be caused by a specific event such as the death of a loved one, or it may be caused by a chemical or hormonal imbalance, prescription drugs, alcohol, physical illness, or psychological factors. Depression may be treated with medication and/or counseling or therapy.

Dermatologist: A physician who specializes in the diagnosis and treatment of skin diseases.

Direct Admissions: Refers to the admission of residents from outside a residential facility directly to the nursing unit. Some facilities restrict the use of their nursing units to residents of their independent-living or assisted-living sections.

Donor Card: A card carried by individuals expressing their wish to donate all or parts of their bodies (such as tissues and organs for transplantation) in the case of death.

Durable Medical Equipment: Reusable medical equipment appropriate for home use, such as wheelchairs and oxygen equipment.

Durable Power of Attorney for Health Care: A legal document in which an individual names another person as attorney-in-fact and authorizes that person to make health-care decisions on his or her behalf in *any* situation in which the individual is unable to make his or her own decisions. The attorney-in-fact can make decisions not just in the event of a terminal illness or irreversible coma, but also in the case of a reversible coma or other temporary situation, as well as in the case of mental incompetence. The individual may also express in this document his or her wishes regarding medical treatment, including the use of life-sustaining measures.

Elimination Period: The length of time the insured has to wait before the insurance company will begin paying benefits. For example, coverage for hospitalization may not begin until the seventh day of each hospital stay. The shorter the elimination period, the more expensive the premium will be. (See also **Waiting Period**.)

Emergency Call System: A system operated by button, pull cord, switch, remote, or telephone that allowed residents to call for help in case of an emergency. Emergency call systems are usually installed in bedrooms and/or bathrooms.

Endowment Fee: See **Entrance Fee**.

Enrollment Period: A specific amount of time during which an individual may enroll in Medicare without risk of surcharges for late enrollment or delays in coverage. A person's initial enrollment period is a seven-month period that begins three months before the month he or she first becomes eligible for Medicare.

Entrance Fee: An upfront, lump-sum fee that some residential facilities charge residents to enter the facility. Depending on the facility, the entrance fee may be fully refundable, partially refundable or nonrefundable if the resident moves or dies. There are three basic types of entrance fee contracts (see **Extensive Contract, Modified Contract**, and **Fee-for-Service Contract**), which relate to the amount of service and health care included. Regardless of the type of contract, residents also pay a monthly fee.

Exclusions: Specified items *not* covered by an insurance policy. Exclusions are listed in the policy. For example, cosmetic surgery is a typical exclusion in health insurance policies.

Extensive Contract: A type of entrance fee contract that provides shelter, all services provided by the facility, and unlimited health care. In addition to paying a lump-sum entrance fee, residents pay a monthly fee. (Also called *all-inclusive contract*.)

Family Practitioner: A physician who provides comprehensive medical services to patients, and often their family members, of all ages on an ongoing basis.

Fee-for-Service: Refers to the traditional system of health-care delivery in which a doctor or other provider is paid a fee for a service rendered.

Fee-for-Service Contract: A type of entrance fee contract that provides shelter, basic service, and access to nursing care. The entrance fee and monthly fee are lower than with an extensive or modified contract, but residents pay a full per diem rate for nursing care. Residents pay additional charges (fee-for-service) for meals and other services, such as transportation and housekeeping, that are included in extensive or modified contracts.

Financial Statement: A report containing financial information about an individual or company, including income, assets, and liabilities during a given accounting period. (See also **Balance Sheet** and **Income Statement**.)

Flat Percentage Refund: The amount of money refunded is figured on the basis of a flat percentage at a given period of time. For example, 80 percent of a deposit is refunded during the first year, 70 percent during the second year, and so on.

Founder's Fee: See **Entrance Fee**.

Frail Elderly: Refers to people seventy-five years and older with physical limitations caused by chronic health problems.

Free-Look Period: In most states a person buying insurance is given a specified period of time (usually ten to thirty days) to look over a policy with the right to cancel and get a full refund.

Functional Impairment: Any reduction in a person's ability to perform the activities of daily living, such as eating, bathing, dressing, grooming, going to the toilet, and walking.

Gatekeepers: Insurance policy restrictions that limit conditions under which the insured is eligible to received certain benefits. For example, a policy may cover care in a skilled-nursing facility, but have a gatekeeper that says that such care must be required as a result of sickness or injury (which would exclude custodial care).

Geriatrics: The branch of medicine and nursing that deals with the diseases of old age.

Geriatric Care Manager: A professional (with a masters-degree level of training in gerontology, social work, nursing, or counseling) who specializes in assisting seniors and their families with long-term care.

Geriatrician: A physician specializing in the treatment of elderly patients.

Gerontology: The study of the causes and consequences of aging and old age.

Geropsychology: The study of the behavior of elderly people.

Glaucoma: A buildup of fluid in the eye that causes excessive pressure to the optic nerve. The optic nerve becomes damaged, resulting in partial or complete vision loss.

Guaranteed Renewable: A noncancelable insurance policy that guarantees the insured the right to renew the policy until he or she reaches a certain age. The insurance company can increase premiums but cannot cancel the policy unless the insured fails to pay the premium, or unless all policies of that type are canceled in a geographical area or everywhere.

Health Care Financing Administration (HCFA): The federal agency responsible for oversight of Medicare and Medicaid. HCFA is a unit of the Department of Health and Human Services.

Health Care Proxy: See **Durable Power of Attorney for Health Care.**

Health Maintenance Organization (HMO): A prepaid health plan that provides preventative care and medical services to members (usually called subscribers) for a fixed premium. Some plans call for small deductibles and/or nominal copayments, but basically the premium covers whatever amount of care the member receives. Members are limited, however, to using only physicians and facilities affiliated with the HMO. The HMO may have its own salaried physicians or may contract with group practices or private-practice physicians to provide health care to its members. Medicare coverage was expanded in 1985 to allow Medicare beneficiaries to enroll in HMOs that have a contract with Medicare.

Home Health Agency: A private or public agency that provides nursing care, therapy, and other types of health-care services in the home.

Home Health Care: Nursing care, therapy, and other types of health-care services provided for patients at home.

Homemaker Services: A type of home health-care service that includes cooking, cleaning, and other housekeeping chores.

Hospice: A program of noncurative care that includes pain relief, symptom management, and support for terminally ill patients and their families. The goal of hospice is to let patients die at home with as little pain as possible, but, if necessary, care can be provided in an inpatient hospice unit, hospital, or nursing facility.

Income: Any money received, such as wages, pensions, cash benefits, and rent from income-producing property. The amount of your income and the value of your assets (with some exclusions) determine your eligibility for Medicaid.

Income Statement: A statement of an individual's or company's income, profits, and losses during a particular accounting period.

Incontinence: Lack of voluntary control over the bladder and/or bowels.

Independent Living: Refers to the ability of active and healthy seniors to live independently without assistance. A residential facility may be all independent living or may have different levels of care with a separate independent-living section for seniors who are able to live on their own in apartments, condominiums, cottages, or some other housing arrangement. The facility may offer services and amenities for the convenience of the residents, but these services are not necessary for the residents to be able to function on a daily basis.

Inflation Protection Clause: A clause in an insurance policy that provides for increases in benefit amounts each year.

Informed Consent: A right of all patients to provide or withhold their consent to any medical procedure after the procedure and the risks involved have been carefully explained.

Inpatient Care: Care provided in a medical facility where the patient has been admitted for overnight stay.

Intensive Care Unit (ICU): A hospital unit staffed twenty-four hours with specially trained personnel that is specially equipped to provide continuous vital sign monitoring of patients who are seriously ill or coming out of major surgery.

Intermediate-Care Facility (ICF): A type of nursing facility that provides twenty-four-hour basic medical care for patients who need recuperative and rehabilitative care. More intensive medical procedures, such as intravenous therapy or feeding tubes, are *not* provided. Care is provided under the supervision of a registered nurse.

Intravenous Therapy: The slow and controlled administration of fluids and nutrients to a patient through a small tube inserted in the patient's vein.

License: A document granting legal permission to do something specific. Nursing facilities must be licensed by the state to operate.

Licensed Practical Nurse (LPN): A nurse who is licensed by the state to provide personal care and to administer certain technical procedures to patients under the supervision of a registered nurse. LPNs must complete a one-year nursing program and pass a state licensing examination.

Licensure: The procedure by which an individual or facility receives a license after completing the necessary requirements.

Lien: A legal claim on someone else's property as security for an unpaid debt.

Life-Care Community: A particular type of continuing-care retirement community that offers only an extensive type of entrance-fee contract (a resident pays a lump-sum fee to enter, plus monthly fees, and in return is guaranteed shelter, services, and health care for the remainder of his or her life).

Life Support: The use of artificial means, such as a respirator, to keep a person alive.

Lifetime Reserve Days: Medicare beneficiaries have a reserve of sixty days that can be used once in their lifetime for inpatient hospital care once Medicare coverage runs out. Once deductibles are met, Medicare will pay all or a portion of eligible hospital charges for ninety days per benefit period. Patients who stay longer than ninety days may use all or some of their reserve days to extend their Medicare coverage.

Living Will: A legal document in which an individual expresses his or her desire not to be kept alive by artificial means or "heroic measures" in the event of a terminal illness or an irreversible coma. The document can prohibit specific medical treatments or all life-sustaining measures. Living will requirements vary by state. A living will is one type of advance directive. (See also **Durable Power of Attorney for Health Care.**)

Long-Term Care: A comprehensive range of services (including medical care, custodial care, and a variety of social services) provided over a long period of time for elderly, chronically ill, or disabled individuals in a licensed facility.

Long-Term-Care Insurance: A type of insurance policy sold by private insurance companies to cover the cost of custodial care provided in a nursing home or in an individual's home by a home health-care agency. Health insurance pays medical expenses, while long-term-care insurance pays for caregiving.

Macular Degeneration: Degeneration of the central area of the retina resulting in a blind spot in the central field of vision. It is a progressive disorder common in the elderly.

Medicaid: A state-run medical assistance program that pays the cost of medical care for people of all ages with low income and low assets. Medicaid, unlike Medicare, will pay for long-term nursing care.

Medical Director: A licensed physician who supervises medical care at a skilled-nursing facility. The physician must be on call and available to the facility twenty-four hours a day but usually spends only a limited number of hours each week on the premises. The director also acts as the liaison between the administrator of a nursing facility and the attending physicians of individual patients.

Medically Needy: A determination of Medicaid eligibility. A person whose income is above the Medicaid limit, but whose medical costs are high, is deemed medically needy if his or her net income falls below the Medicaid limit once medical expenses are subtracted.

Medicare: A federal health insurance program for people sixty-five and older regardless of income, and certain disabled people regardless of age. Medicare also serves people with permanent kidney disease regardless of age. Medicare pays only a portion of a beneficiary's medical expenses; the beneficiary pays deductibles and copayments. Medicare is divided into two parts: Part A (hospital insurance) is premium free; Part B (medical insurance) is voluntary and requires payment of a monthly premium.

Medicare Allowable Amount: See **Medicare Approved Amount.**

Medicare Approved Amount: An amount determined by Medicare to be a reasonable charge for a specific medical service. After deductibles are met, Medicare pays 80 percent of the approved amount, and the Medicare beneficiary is responsible for the remaining 20 percent (called coinsurance).

Medicare Carrier: A commercial insurance company that contracts with the Health Care Financing Administration to process Medicare Part B claims and make Medicare payments for services by physicians and suppliers.

Medication Management: A service provided by most assisted-living facilities that includes the storage of residents' medication, reminders to residents to take their medication, oversight of residents taking their medication, and medication record keeping.

Most states prohibit unlicensed personnel from actually giving medication to residents.

Medigap: A term that refers to a variety of Medicare supplemental insurance policies sold by private insurance companies. Medigap policies fill in the gaps of Medicare coverage by paying certain charges that Medicare beneficiaries otherwise would pay out-of-pocket. All Medigap policies must, by law, include certain benefits.

MEDPARD Directory: The short name for the *Medicare Participating Physicians and Suppliers Directory,* which lists doctors and suppliers who participate in the Medicare system and who accept Medicare assignment. The directory is available from your state Medicare carrier.

Mobility: The ability to move. Elderly people with decreased mobility may need assistance with dressing or other physical tasks.

Modified Contract: A type of entrance fee contract that includes the cost of shelter, services, amenities, and a limited number of days of nursing care. After those days are used up the resident pays a monthly or daily rate for nursing care.

Monthly Maintenance Fee: A monthly fee paid by condominium owners for the maintenance of common areas such as lobbies, stairways, hallways, elevators, and grounds.

National Institutes of Health (NIH): A group of medical research organizations and a research hospital operating under the Department of Health and Human Services.

Nephrologist: A physician who specializes in the diagnosis and treatment of kidney disease.

No Code: An order given by the physician of a terminally ill patient (according to the wishes of the patient or the patient's family) that means "do not resuscitate" or do not undertake heroic measures to save the patient's life. The "no code" order may be written on the patient's hospital chart or given verbally to the hospital staff.

Non-forfeiture Benefit: An optional insurance benefit that provides for a partial refund if a policy is dropped after a certain number of years without the insured ever having used any of the policy's coverage.

Non-participating Provider: A health-care provider that has chosen not to participate in the Medicare system and, therefore, does not accept assignment (accept the Medicare-approved amount as payment in full for services rendered). Medicare patients who use the services of a nonparticipating provider must pay the provider's full bill, then file a claim with Medicare for reimbursement of 80 percent of the amount that Medicate has approved as a reasonable charge for that service.

Nonprofit Facility: A residential facility legally structured to require that all profits made by the facility must be put back into the facility and to prohibit the distribution of any of the facility's income to directors, officers, or members.

Nonrefundable: Refers to a type of entrance-fee contract in which none of the entrance fee will be paid back or refunded to a resident or the resident's estate in the event that the resident decides to move out of the facility or dies while residing there.

Non-renewable: A type of insurance policy that cannot be renewed after the period of time for which it was written. Also called *term* insurance.

Nurse Assistant: A person who assists residents with personal care such as bathing, going to the toilet, dressing, and other nonmedical procedures, under the supervision of a registered nurse or licensed practical nurse. Nurse assistants who work in nursing facilities certified by Medicare and Medicaid must be trained and certified. A nurse assistant may also be called an *aide*.

Nursing Care: The highest level of care that may be provided in a residential facility. There are different levels of nursing care: custodial (basic supervision and assistance with personal needs), intermediate (basic medical care), and skilled (more intensive medical care).

Occupational Therapy: Therapy designed to help physically or mentally disabled individuals learn to adapt to their limitations by using specific strategies and/or assistive devices.

Oncologist: A physician who specializes in the diagnosis and treatment of cancer.

Operating Budget: A listing of anticipated income and expenses for a stated time.

Ophthalmologist: A physician who specializes in the diagnosis and treatment (including surgery) of eye disorders. An ophthalmologist also tests vision and prescribed corrective lens.

Optician: One who makes or sells eyeglasses and contact lenses. An optician cannot test eyes or prescribe lens.

Optionally Renewable: A type of insurance policy that can be renewed at the discretion of the insurance company.

Optometrist: A professional who examines and tests eyes and prescribes corrective lens. An optometrist is not a physician.

Orthopedist: A physician who specializes in the diagnosis and treatment of disorders of bones, joints, and related structures such as muscle, tendons, and ligaments.

Outpatient Care: Medical care given in a clinic or other medical facility to patients who are not admitted to the hospital for an overnight stay.

Parkinson's Disease: A brain disorder caused by nerve cell degeneration in a certain part of the brain that results in a deficiency of dopamine, a chemical substance that helps transmit nerve impulses. The chief symptoms are tremors, slow movements, stiffness, a shuffling walk, and difficulty with balance.

Partially Refundable: Refers to a type of entrance fee contract in which a portion of the entrance fee is refunded to the resident or the resident's estate if the resident moves out of the facility or dies while residing at the facility. The refund amount is usually figured on the basis of a flat percentage or declining scale. (See also **Flat Percentage Refund** and **Declining Balance Refund.**)

Participating Provider: A health-care provider who has chosen to participate in the Medicare system, thus agreeing to accept assignment (accept as payment in full the amount approved by Medicare as a reasonable charge for a particular service.) Once deductibles are met, Medicare pays 80 percent of that approved amount directly to the provider, and the Medicare beneficiary pays the remaining 20 percent coinsurance.

Per Diem: Daily.

Personal Care: Services provided to assist residents with the activities of daily living (dressing, bathing, grooming, eating, mobility). Many assisted-living facilities are called personal-care homes. The legal definitions may vary from state to state, but the concept of assisted living and personal care are basically the same.

Physical Therapy: A program of treatment designed to help relieve pain, restore particular functions, and strengthen muscles following an illness or injury.

Physical Restraints: Devices used as a protective measure to limit someone's movement in a bed or chair. Typical restraints include bed side rails, harnesses, and straps, which might be used to prevent a weak, unsteady person from getting out of bed and falling or to prevent an unconscious patient from pulling at tubes or bandages.

Podiatrist: A professional who deals with the care and treatment of feet.

Preexisting Condition: A health problem or medical condition that existed before an insurance policy was purchased. The policy will exclude coverage for that condition for a specific amount of time (called a waiting period).

Preoccupancy Reservation Deposit: See **Waiting List Deposit.**

Premium: The amount paid for an insurance policy. The premium may be paid by the insured or the insured's employer.

Private Duty Nurse: A registered nurse hired and paid directly by patients.

Provider: A person such as a doctor, technician, or therapist who provides medical services; a place such as a hospital or clinic that provides medical services; or a supplier of medical equipment.

Psychiatrist: A physician who specializes in treating mental, emotional, and behavioral disorders using counseling, therapy, and/or medication.

Radiologist: A physician who specializes in the use of X rays, ultrasound, MRI, nuclear imaging, and radioactive substances to diagnose and treat medical problems.

Recuperative Care: Care needed for a patient to get well again following an illness, injury, or surgery.

Refundable: Refers to a type of entrance-fee contract in which the entrance fee will be paid back or refunded to a resident or the resident's estate in the event that the resident decides to move out of the facility or dies while residing there. (See also **Partially Refundable** and **Nonrefundable.**

Registered Dietician (RD): A person educated about nutrition and its effects on the body, who either counsels individual clients about their dietary needs or manages and supervises the dietary needs of a facility.

Registered Nurse (RN): A nurse licensed by the state to perform the widest range of nursing services. A RN has the highest level of education of all nurses.

Rehabilitative Care: Care aimed at restoring a patient's health and ability to function following an illness, injury, surgery, or period of substance abuse.

Renewable: Refers to a type of insurance policy that the insured can renew for life at his or her discretion.

Rent: A fixed payment made by a resident, usually on a monthly basis, for the occupancy and use of a specified living space.

Request for Earnings and Benefit Estimate Statement: Individuals can find out if they or their spouse have enough work credits under the Social Security system to be eligible for Medicare by filling out this form and mailing it to the processing center listed on the form. The form is available from your local Social Security offices.

Rescission: Most states have a rescission law giving consumers the right to revoke or cancel certain contractual agreements within a specified amount of time (varying typically from three to ninety days).

Residential Care: Includes room, board, and assistance with activities of daily living (eating, dressing, bathing, grooming, going to the toilet, walking, and taking medication). Some states use *residential care* as the legal term to refer to assisted living.

Respite Care: Care provided on a short-term basis for someone unable to care for himself or herself for the purpose of providing temporary relief for that person's caretaker. Respite care for terminally ill patients is often provided at an inpatient hospice facility.

Rheumatologist: A physician who specializes in the diagnosis and treatment of diseases of the joints, muscles, and connective tissues.

Scheduled Transportation: A service provided at many residential facilities that includes car, bus, or minivan transportation for residents to particular locations (such as a nearby grocery, mall, and bank) at scheduled times during the day.

Security Deposit: A partial payment made in advance to insure against any damage to a residential unit. Normal wear and tear are not considered damage. If there is no damage, 100 percent of the security deposit should be refunded when the unit is vacated.

Semiprivate Room: A room with no more than two beds.

Sheltered Care: Includes room, board, supervision, and assistance with activities of daily living (eating, bathing, dressing, grooming, walking, going to the toilet, and taking medication). Some states use *sheltered care* as the legal term to refer to assisted living.

Skilled-nursing Facility (SNF): Licensed by the state to provide twenty-four-hour comprehensive nursing services on a short-term or long-term basis. Skilled-nursing facilities have at least one registered nurse on duty during the day. Care is provided under the supervision of a licensed physician, who may be on call. A skilled-nursing facility is staffed and equipped to provide subacute care, which is the highest degree of care outside of a hospital. Skilled-nursing care is more intense medical care than intermediate care.

Social Worker: A person (usually with a master's degree in social work) who provides counseling services to clients and their families and also links clients with other services available in the community.

Speech Therapy: A program of treatment and exercises designed to help people with speech and language problems.

Spend Down: Refers to a process by which a nursing home resident becomes eligible for Medicaid by using his or her assets to pay for medical and nursing care until those assets are reduced or "spent down" below the state's Medicaid limit.

Sponsor: A corporation, partnership, or association with tax-exempt status that has an association with a nonprofit residential facility. Churches, civic associations, and fraternal orders are typical sponsors. The sponsor may or may not have some financial or legal obligation to the facility.

Subacute Care: The type of comprehensive nursing care provided in a skilled-nursing facility. Subacute care is the next step down from hospital or acute care.

Subscribers: Members enrolled in a Health Maintenance Organization plan.

Term Insurance: See **Nonrenewable.**

Transferring: (1) Refers to a permanent or temporary move from one level of care to another in a residential facility. (2) Refers to moving an individual to and from a bed, chair, or wheelchair.

Waiting List Deposit: A partial payment made to have your name put on a facility's waiting list. (Also called a *preoccupancy reservation deposit.*)

Waiting Period: Refers the amount of time you have to wait after buying an insurance policy before coverage begins. For example, your policy may state that coverage begins one month after you sign the policy. There may also be a long waiting period for coverage of a preexisting condition.

INDEX